CLOSE READING

THE BASICS

Clo   reading is the most essential skill that literature students
con nue to develop across the full length of their studies. This
boo is the ideal guide to the practice, providing a methodology
that an be used for poetry, novels, drama, and beyond. Using
class works of literature, such as *Hamlet* and *The Great Gatsby* as
case   tudies, David Greenham presents a unique, contextual
app: ach to close reading, while addressing key questions such as:

- What is close reading?
- What is the importance of the relationships between words?
- How can close reading enhance reading pleasure?
- s there a method of close reading that works for all literary
  genres?
- How can close reading unlock complexity?
- How does the practice of close reading relate to other theo-
  retical and critical approaches?

Close Reading: The Basics is formulated to bring together reading
ple sure and analytic techniques that will engage the student of
lite ature and enhance their reading experience.

David Greenham is Associate Professor of English Literature at
the University of the West of England, UK.

The Basics

For a full list of titles in this series, please visit:
www.routledge.com/The-Basics/book-series/B

CLOSE READING

THE BASICS

David Greenham

Routledge
Taylor & Francis Group

LONDON AND NEW YORK

First published 2019
by Routledge
2 Park Square, Milton Park, Abingdon, Oxon OX14 4RN

and by Routledge
711 Third Avenue, New York, NY 10017

Routledge is an imprint of the Taylor & Francis Group, an informa business

© 2019 David Greenham

British Library Cataloguing in Publication Data
A catalogue record for this book is available from the British Library

Library of Congress Cataloging in Publication Data
A catalog record has been requested for this book

ISBN: 978-1-138-56219-6 (hbk)
ISBN: 978-1-138-56222-6 (pbk)
ISBN: 978-0-203-70997-9 (ebk)

Typeset in Bembo
by Taylor & Francis Books
Printed in Great Britain by CPI Group (UK) Ltd, Croydon, CR0 4YY

CONTENTS

PREFACE

When done well close reading can look like critical magic: an interpretation of a poem or play appearing like the white rabbit from a top hat. But how is it done? This is a question I've asked myself many times; it's also a question that my students have often asked me. It's a tough question to answer because there has never been a *single* book that I could point to and say: '*that's* how it's done!' The best examples of close reading are scattered across dozens of different books, essays and chapters from almost a hundred years of criticism. They are written by different people with different aims and approaches. Some tackle prose or plays; most tackle poetry. This has too long left the student to wander amidst a labyrinth of disconnected possibilities, where there are many examples, but no clear guidance. I set out to write this book with the express purpose of providing a single place where any 'magic' that there is in close reading could be brought out into the open and its secret paths made available to the widest possible number of interested readers.

This is not to say that critics haven't thought long and hard about close reading and offered theories to support their practice. The method worked out in this guide is in part an attempt to turn a number of insights from I. A. Richards, the founder of close reading as an academic practice in the 1920s, into usable tools. The most significant aspect of Richards' approach to literature is that meaning is not inherent *in* individual words but is rather derived from the relationships *between* words (which he calls 'inter-inanimation'). As you'll see, the method I put forward here is a thoroughgoing development of this basic insight. Before Richards brought his critical practice to the university, Robert Graves and Laura Riding had unearthed vital discoveries in their work on the multiple meanings of Shakespeare's sonnets and modernist poetry in the 1920s. In 1930, Richards' student, William Empson, showed just how far literary interpretation could go in his peerless *Seven Types of Ambiguity*. Their 'Practical Criticism' focused on the words on the page, and more specifically the different kinds of meaning that language's essential ambiguities, generated by the relationships between words, throw up. In this context, ambiguity does not mean vagueness. Ambiguity, for the close reader, is the rigorous and responsible (though often still playful) application of their interpretative power. As the American essayist Ralph Waldo Emerson put it, almost a century before Richards, 'There is … creative reading, as well as creative writing. When the mind is braced by labour and invention, the page of whatever book we read becomes luminous with manifold allusion' ('The American Scholar'). That there is play and pleasure in close reading as a creative act should not be ignored or underestimated. It is one of the foundations of this book.

The kinds of readings put forward by the Practical Critics were picked up and further theorised by the American 'New Critics' such as W. K. Wimsatt, Cleanth Brooks, John Crowe Ransom, Allen Tate, and Rueben Brower. Their often highly technical close readings became the models for, and the mainstays of, the teaching of English literature from the 1940s to the 1980s, in such classic works as Brooks and Robert Penn Warren's 1938 *Understanding Poetry* (which is still in print), Brooks' own 1947 *The Well Wrought Urn*, and Brower's 1951 *The Fields of Light*. This was, though, very much practice by example rather than by replicable method. In the 1970s and 1980s, close reading largely ceased to be an end in itself. Instead it became a grounding practice for the rich and often politically and ethically charged criticism undertaken by a wide range of literary and critical theorists, such as Roland Barthes, Jacques Derrida, Julia Kristeva, and Homi Bhabha. Other insightful and brilliant critics, such as Christopher Ricks and Helen Vendler, maintained the traditional practices of the Practical and New Critics and passed them on to generations of readers. What these diverse and often conflicting interpreters of literature have in common is a persistent interest in language's potential for multiple

meanings and the rich readings that can be won from understanding this. But there has never, even implicitly, been a shared
methodological approach to their varying practices. What follows
is an attempt to abstract from this vast body of work a useable,
basic, stage-by-stage, methodology for close reading that can
enable the student of literature to perform at least a little of their
critical 'magic'.

I would like to acknowledge the critical practice of each of the
above critics, whose work has influenced me in ways that I cannot
fully account for in this book. Other important precursors will be
found in the Further Reading sections of each chapter. Influence, of
course, does not equal responsibility. Some of these critics might
struggle to see themselves or their work in the book that follows.
Nevertheless, I hope there is always some connection in spirit. I'd
also like to acknowledge the insights that have been provided by the
teaching of my colleagues at the University of the West of England.
In particular, Professor Peter Rawlings, Dr Kerry Sinanan, and Dr
Britta Martens, whose lectures on *Hamlet* and e. e. cummings were
invaluable. I'd also like to thank Dr Zoe Brennan for reading and
commenting on an early draft. Additionally, I'd like to thank the last
ten years of students who have trusted me to refine aspects of my
method in my lectures and seminars. Finally, I'd like to thank Dr
Jennifer Lewis for reading multiple versions of this book and for
providing unstinting support along the way.

INTRODUCTION

One must be an inventor to read well.

Ralph Waldo Emerson, 'The American Scholar'

Reading is one of the strangest and most powerful of all human experiences. We look at a few marks on a page and, out of them, we make worlds and populate them; we anticipate futures for people and creatures that have never existed; we hear voices, feel emotions, touch the past, learn about the deepest aspects of human nature; we take part in adventures, closely observe the most mundane of social encounters, watch people fall in love, witness pain and suffering, elation and achievement; sometimes we are disturbed or unsettled, we may even become baffled, or get bogged down – then it's a personal triumph to have got through that story at all. The list of the effects of reading could go on and on, as those marks on the page are unique to every book we read. But what is most remarkable about reading, and what draws so many people to it on a daily basis, is that those few marks on the page are able to deliver so much pleasure. The pleasure of escape, of having experiences unavailable in everyday life, of meeting new people, of being elevated by an encounter with a writer's brilliant language, of glimpsing something unexpected about the world, of everything suddenly making sense, of a shattering twist, of being caught up in a runaway plot, of re-reading and coming to feel like a book is your very own – again, the list could go on and on. To create this all we appear to have done is move our eyes along a long line of letters. Though clearly that is not quite *all* that is happening when we read. So what *does* happen when we read?

Why *do* we enjoy reading? How *can* we understand reading, and by understanding it *enjoy* it even more? These are some of the questions that will be answered in this book.

CAN ANALYSIS BE PLEASURABLE TOO?

There's a belief, and it's widely held, that the analysis of pleasure somehow spoils pleasure, as if a fuller understanding of what is enjoyable would correspondingly diminish its effect. This goes hand in hand with the idea that enjoyment is spontaneous: in and of the moment. Spontaneous and intuitive pleasures are, of course, rich and of significant value. But it is the contention of this book that such pleasures (like those listed above) can be enhanced with attention to what it is that created them – that is, by *analysis*. Analysis means, if we take it back to its original usage, the 'act of resolving (something) into its elements' (*OED*). It comes from a long-held idea that in order to understand something we have to take it apart and then put it back together again with, ideally, new insights in place. In terms of our response to literature's pleasures this remains problematic if we hold to the idea that the appreciation of, say, a poem should be spontaneous: just how it makes us feel. As William Wordsworth, himself a poet, once put it: 'We murder to dissect'. Pleasure, his poem implies, is derived from direct intuition and 'Our meddling intellect/Mis-shapes the beauteous forms of things' (*Lyrical Ballads*, 81).

Nevertheless, I would want to ask how far we *really* enjoy anything we don't have a pretty good understanding of – for example, sport or music (and Wordsworth certainly understood poetry!). We usually need to get the *rules* of sport or understand the *type* of music to appreciate it, and our enjoyment of either of these tends to drive us to understand more, say about tradition and context; even to be competitive in our knowledge. Many people already feel that about literature – especially the type of people likely to undertake serious literary study. But a certain wariness persists: the sense that analysis may be difficult, and that as difficulty creeps in the pleasures of reading creep out. What precisely is at stake here? Well, I would say again that *intuitive* pleasure is valuable – essential even – as it attracts the reader *toward* literature in the first place; but what's really valuable for a *student* of literature is 'analytic pleasure'. Analytic pleasure is the feeling you get as a reader when your intuition has been enhanced by a method that offers a more intense understanding of a literary work. Not only does this give you as a reader a better sense of how your initial pleasure came about, but, more importantly, it allows for entirely new pleasures founded on the skilful practice of close reading. So, far from Wordsworth's contention that the intellect 'mis-shapes' beauty, analytic pleasure *re*-shapes 'the beauteous forms of things' into richer and, because better understood, more profound forms.

IN THE BEGINNING IS THE WORD

The words 'analysis' and 'pleasure', then, are only at first strange bedfellows. When put together they inevitably transform each other because words, when connected, can't help but affect each other's meanings. Indeed, that's how *meaning* works (and, as you'll see, it's also how this book works). No word, however clearly it is articulated, has a discernible meaning outside of a specific *context*. The practice of close reading begins with that understanding: words get their meanings by working together. Words, individually, are unfixed and unsettled because most of them (possibly all of them) have more than one possible interpretation. Thus, any word outside of a particular context has *too much* potential meaning. The context in which a word appears shrinks that potential usually to one meaning and sometimes, where ambiguity remains, to two or more meanings.

As an example, let's look at the word 'word' itself. It has a variety of senses, amongst which, without for the time being reaching for the dictionary, should be included:

1   a collection of letters that have meaning (the written word)
2   a collection of sounds that have meaning (the spoken word)
3   a promise (I give you my word)
4   something said on behalf of another (I'll put a good word in for you),
5   an indication of surprise (my word!)
6   something with scriptural authority (the word of God)
7   a report or news (I'll send word when I get there), and so on.

On its own, the word 'word' always has *all* of this potential, but the context usually limits it to one possibility. We can think about how this works by looking at the following sentence:

> Close reading is about enjoying the way the words on the page create beauty in complexity.

We could slot each of the above meanings for 'word' into this sentence as follows:

1   Close reading is about enjoying the way the [**collections of letters**] on the page create beauty in complexity.
2   Close reading is about enjoying the way [**collections of sounds**] on the page create beauty in complexity.
3   Close reading is about enjoying the way the [**promises**] on the page create beauty in complexity.
4   Close reading is about enjoying the way the [**things said on behalf of another**] on the page create beauty in complexity.
5   Close reading is about enjoying the way the [**surprises**] on the page create beauty in complexity.
6   Close reading is about enjoying the way the [**scriptural authority**] on the page creates beauty in complexity.
7   Close reading is about enjoying the way the [**news**] on the page creates beauty in complexity.

So which options are most likely? Well, the first is the one that makes most sense: 'Close reading is about enjoying the way [**the collections of letters**] on the page create beauty in complexity.' Though, if we look at the range of uses again, there is the possibility that meaning 2, **collections of sounds**, especially in the case of verse and drama, may be relevant (and as we shall see in Chapter 6, it certainly is). Interestingly, uses 5 and 6 could also make sense, though they are unlikely. A case could even be made for 3 (consider a poem about the 'promises' of love, for example). Indeed, given the right context *any* of these senses could be made to work. Of course, this isn't the way we normally think about language. Generally   we   appear   to   choose   our   meanings spontaneously. Even so, when it comes to selecting between these various possibilities it is *context* that determines that choice of meaning through limitation. However, as we shall see, literary language often demands that the echoes of the other meanings of words come into play – this is part of what makes literary language pleasurable. And, even if the writer has not explicitly urged it, good criticism may well find that 'creative' meaning happens when words are opened up in just the right way by the practice of careful close reading.

COMPLEXITY CASE STUDY

Throughout this guide you'll find several short 'complexity case studies' in which I take a tricky example of literary language and work it through using the aspect of close reading under discussion. This first one looks at the variations of the use of the word 'word' in a section from Shakespeare's *Romeo and Juliet* (a play that we'll be returning to).

In the famous Act 2 balcony scene Juliet, dismayed at her love for Romeo, a Montague and thus one of her family's bitter enemies, says 'That which we call a rose/By any other word would smell as sweet' (2.2.43–4). In this speech meanings 1 and 2 of 'word' are in place: a word is a collection of letters and/or sounds with a particular referent. It's a little more complex than that (as usual with Shakespeare) because the referent, 'rose', is being used to figure 'Montague'. Juliet's claim, then, is that a foul name cannot change the essential qualities of a beautiful thing (just how metaphors like this work will be the subject of Chapter 3). When, a few lines later, Romeo responds to Juliet's profession of love by saying 'I take thee at thy word' (2.2.49), meaning 3 is being referred to – word as a promise. But, because we are using our close reading skills to attend to repetitions, the resonances of the earlier meaning are there too. Juliet's promise of love (her word), then, now begins to 'rename' Romeo (the word that names him): 'I'll be new baptis'd' he says. More interestingly still, word is now taking on the 'holy' significance of meaning 6, as it will later in Act 2 with reference to the 'holy words' of the marriage ceremony. Following this,

> Romeo rejects the 'word' that names him: 'Had I it written, I would tear the word' (2.2.57). The meaning of 'word' is now clearly meaning 1, a collection of letters – but by this time just what the word 'word' refers to has become highly complex and delightfully ambiguous: it's an old name, it's a new name, it's a promise, it's holy, it's something that can be destroyed ...

Complexities like these can often be found when the context allows for more than one meaning for any given word to be at work within a literary text. Developing a taste for this kind of ambiguity is one of the great pleasures of reading literature, as you'll see in the first chapter of this book. Giving you the skills to produce this kind of reading is my aim.

SUMMARY

In miniature, the process just outlined is the foundation of the method of analysis that will be put forward in this guide: there is no meaning without context and thus understanding the fullest range of plausible contexts will offer the most rewarding reading experience. It is in part an incremental process; but ultimately it is a simultaneous one. As such, this is not a guide that can just be 'dipped into' – at least not on a first reading. Rather this guide gradually outlines a holistic methodology for the practice of close reading that begins with your initial intuitive pleasure in reading, then refines this by focusing on individual words (as we've just seen), before moving out to sentences, and then out to paragraphs, stanzas or chapters, then to the whole of a text, finally moving even further out to the concerns of the world: its politics, its history and its contemporary preoccupations.

The method that you will learn in order to achieve this is based on six basic **contexts of close reading**, each of which can be understood as a way of analysing literary language in itself, but which will be introduced incrementally across the chapters of this book. These six contexts of close reading are as follows:

THE SIX CONTEXTS OF CLOSE READING

1 The semantic: what individual words can mean (Chapter 2);
2 The syntactic: how words mean things when they are put together (Chapter 3);
3 The thematic: how themes emerge and affect meanings when we read (Chapters 3 and 4);
4 The iterative: the ways that repetition and patterning affect textual meanings (Chapters 5 and 6);
5 The generic: how the kind of work we are reading changes our approach to its meanings (Chapter 7);
6 The adversarial: how historical, political and theoretical concerns reshape meanings (Chapter 8).

However, before I begin to work through these basic contexts of close reading in detail, it's important to return to the foundational idea of *reading pleasure*. It is in pleasure that our reading begins. But our pleasure is actually created by an unconscious understanding of the basic contexts. So, what I want to show is that these contexts are already at work *for* us, and that a better grasp of them can enrich your enjoyment and extend your appreciation of literature. The first chapter, then, concerns the pleasures of reading.

SEVEN PLEASURES OF READING

PLEASURE 1: BEGINNINGS

A well-known book begins as follows:

> In a hole in the ground there lived a hobbit. Not a nasty, dirty, wet hole, filled with the ends of worms and an oozy smell, nor yet a dry, bare, sandy hole with nothing in it to sit down on or to eat: it was a hobbit-hole, and that means comfort.

(11)

Why have these words proven so consistently pleasurable to so many that, even as a child, they'll take the trip into that unknown hole? Well, first, *almost* every word makes immediate sense, creates easily imagined pictures and associations and thus a recognisable space. It also appeals to the senses: sight, touch, smell. The phrasing is nicely balanced, more or less rhythmical ('In a *hole*/in the *ground*'); and the gently iterated negations ('not', 'nor', 'nothing') take each of our simple familiar mental pictures and feelings and deny their relevance, leaving a wonderful blank space to fill. Enlivening it all is the allure of strangeness contained in that one provocative word, used twice, that in contrast to all the rest will resist instant understanding: 'hobbit'. It's a bit like 'rabbit' and rabbits live in holes, but they live in the holes which are counted out by the storyteller – either wet and filled with the ends of worms or, more likely, dry and bare. A '*hobbit*-hole' is clearly something different from *just* a 'hole'. A hobbit, then, is something new to our reading experience, and we want to go down into its hole to find out just what 'it' is. One further detail in the passage is crucial: when we get there we are told we'll be somewhere comfortable. This brief journey of two sentences takes us away from our own space and delivers us to a safe place – a place of 'comfort' with seats and food. So, by the time we've got to the end of the second sentence, we've forgotten we are reading a book. Instead we are travelling into an environment that is new and yet, along with its strangeness, beguilingly promises safety.

The book carries on in this vein as it develops our picture of this world:

> It had a perfectly round door like a porthole, painted green, with a shiny yellow brass knob in the exact middle. The door opened on to a tube-shaped hall like a tunnel: a very comfortable tunnel without smoke, with panelled walls, and floors tiled and carpeted, provided with polished chairs, and lots of pegs for hats and coats – the hobbit was fond of visitors.
>
> (11)

We are stood at the door, then we are whisked inside and all but asked to take off our hat and coat, and then we look around the tiled and carpeted hall and admire the wood panelling. But there's still some strangeness. The door is 'round'; the hall 'tube-shaped.' This is not, then, a 'human' space – we humans, at least in the modern English-speaking world, tend to use rectangles for our homes. But it is also not made by an animal, as the door is not just round it is 'perfectly' round, with a knob in the 'exact' middle; likewise, the chairs are 'polished.' This is an eminently civilised kind of strangeness. In just a few lines there's something familiar yet different enough to create the necessary frisson for a particular kind of pleasure. As we read we are gently unsettled: just off balance enough to topple into the unfolding story.

Now, most people who enjoy reading will have heard of J. R. R. Tolkien's *The Hobbit*, but the story the book tells will only become familiar through reading it. Not all stories are like that. Some are familiar even before we pick up the book that contains them. They are a part of our cultural store, so to speak. A story that is even more well-known than *The Hobbit* begins as follows:

> Two households both alike in dignity,
> (In fair Verona, where we lay our scene)
> From ancient grudge break to new mutiny,
> Where civil blood makes civil hands unclean.
>
> (1.0.1–4)

While being taken into the strange comforts of Bilbo's hobbit-hole can give us the delights of the new, going back to Verona and the setting of *Romeo and Juliet* takes us into an archetype: a story so recognisable to Western culture that its rediscovery takes some effort. But there are, from the beginning, pleasures to be found, even if they are more hard won. Here it's in the wordplay. For example, in this Prologue the word 'scene' is used in two different ways – the *scene* of Verona as a setting and the *scene* of the play as a play. 'Civil' likewise fragments into the meanings of the 'citizens' whose blood will be spilt and the 'politeness' (civility) that will be rendered unclean. *Romeo and Juliet* is a play about division in a city *and* in a language. The Prologue to the play gives us a new pleasure – that of the *play* of language. Even so, this is hardly primary, and though we may enjoy it, such detail could just as easily pass us by. What really draws us to *Romeo and Juliet* is a sense of fatalism: we know – just as Shakespeare's first audience did – that the 'star-crossed lovers' will 'take their life' (1.0.6); and even if we didn't the Prologue tells us of 'The fearful passage of their death-mark'd love.' (1.0.9) The beginning of this play already contains its end. It is strange how the knowledge of what will happen in a literary work doesn't necessarily detract from our enjoyment. Indeed, it can enhance it, allowing us to enjoy the unfolding tragedy without the shock that the loss of two young lives should create at the close of the play's 'two hours' traffic'. (1.0.12) Re-reading, which enables you to return to a book with a better sense of it each time, is one of reading's chief pleasures.

CONTEXTS OF CLOSE READING: BEGINNINGS

In this first chapter my aim is to relate the pleasures of reading to the **contexts of close reading** that were outlined in the Introduction. These boxes will make that relationship explicit and give you a sense of how the later chapters of this guide will unfold.

Pleasure in these first two examples is derived from the way we grasp the words on the page. The 'Prologue' to *Romeo and Juliet* takes two words, 'scene' and 'civil', and uses their **semantic context** to allow at least two meanings for each word to be at work. The semantic context is, basically, any plausible dictionary definition or relevant usage of a word. Shakespeare's use of it here is deliberately, and enjoyably, ambiguous. Tolkien, on the other hand, has invented a word that has no dictionary definition. Therefore, its semantic context isn't something we know in advance or can just look up. To begin to understand the word 'hobbit' we need to make use of the surrounding words, that is, its **syntactic context**. It is words like 'hole', 'comfort', 'carpeted', 'polished chairs', that, by association, will start to help us to anticipate what the word 'hobbit' may come to mean. That is, our pleasure relies on the determination of the semantic context of 'hobbit' in relation to its syntactic context (more on which in Chapters 2 and 3). Of course, there are other **contexts** that are important. If we think about the **generic context**, we can immediately see how important that is. If we know we are reading a tragedy, such as *Romeo and Juliet*, then an unhappy ending will hardly be a surprise – indeed, it's part of the pleasure. If we know we are reading a fantasy novel, then beginning to think about what hobbits may be no stretch – indeed to meet something new is the whole point. If we came across a hobbit in Darwin's *Origin of Species*, or if Dickens' Tiny Tim turned out to be small with hairy feet, our credulity would be over-stretched and our enjoyment ruined. The generic context, as we'll see in Chapter 7, will inevitably direct our attention and our attitude from the outset of our reading. In fact a work's generic context more than anything else may guide our *expectations* of reading pleasure.

PLEASURE 2: MEETING PEOPLE

So, what *does* live in such a strangely comfortable hole? We learn a few things about 'the hobbit' over its opening pages. His name is the satisfyingly rounded Bilbo Baggins; a name which, once more, mixes the familiar with the odd – Bill is a common name, and there are bags everywhere, so the sounds are everyday. Even so 'Bil*bo*' and 'Bag*gins*' rather throws us off. This mixture of the straight forward and the unusual seems to be becoming a theme. Bilbo himself is strung across these poles. On the one hand, the storyteller tells us, 'You could tell exactly what a Baggins would say on any question without the bother of asking him' (12) and as such he is eminently respectable; but on the other hand, his mother is a Took, and the Tooks (including his mother, Belladonna) not only have 'adventures' they are also said to have 'fairy' blood in their veins. (13) The teller of the tale makes it very clear that what we are beginning to read 'is the story of how a Baggins had an adventure' (12); so we know that both elements of his character, shaped by his inheritance, will compete in what follows and we will enjoy watching them play off against each other. Alongside these personal details, we also learn that hobbits are small (about three feet in height), have curly hair on head *and* feet, like to laugh, eat and tend to be portly; but also that they are wary, have 'long clever brown fingers' (13), and can move silently and all but invisibly when the 'large stupid folk like you and me come blundering along' (12). So, this world isn't so far removed from our own; though hobbits are rarely seen in it.

Almost incidentally, through the reference to fairies in Bilbo's ancestry, we are introduced to the idea of magic; but also to the kind of 'everyday' magic that helps hobbits 'disappear' easily when people stumble upon them. In the subsequent pages we are presented with a 'wizard': Gandalf. His introduction is rather enigmatic: 'If you had heard only a quarter of what I have heard about him, and I have only heard a very little of all there is to hear, you would be prepared for any sort of remarkable tale. Tales and adventures sprouted up all over the place wherever he went' (14). In many ways nothing at all is said here – Gandalf is announced through tempting rumours. But we do get a short description to fill this out: 'He had a tall pointed blue hat, a long grey cloak, a silver scarf over which his long white beard hung down below his waist, and immense black boots' (14). So, this catalyst for adventure, in a familiar wizard's hat, and with a familiar wizard's beard, stands outside Bilbo's round green door in the exact spot that we, as a reader on the threshold, stood just a few minutes earlier (in reading time, anyway):

> 'Good morning!' said Bilbo, and he meant it. The sun was shining, and the grass was very green. But Gandalf looked at him from under long bushy eyebrows that stuck out further than the brim of his shady hat.
> 'What do you mean?' he said. 'Do you wish me a good morning, or mean that it is a good morning whether I want it or not; or that you feel good this morning; or that it is a morning to be good on?'
> 'All of them at once,' said Bilbo.

> (14–15)

Gandalf's role seems to be to unsettle things – that has been made clear by the attractive way that tales and adventures 'sprout up' wherever he goes. But he begins by doing nothing more adventurous than unsettling language (though that may turn out to prove the greatest adventure of all). Saying 'Good morning!' is not meant to elicit any other response than an equally banal echo – even when, as here, it somehow reflects the qualities of the day. Gandalf interrogates it, offering *four* different interpretations of Bilbo's bland greeting; meanwhile staring, with just a touch of threat, from under his remarkably extensive eyebrows. This challenges Bilbo's conventionality, just as it is meant to do. However, Bilbo is quite equal to it, and disarms Gandalf with his pleasant 'All of them at once.' He's not going to let a little ambiguity unsettle him on such a fine morning. Gandalf, though, is also not ready to be put off his stride. He has seen in Bilbo's 'clever' fingers, his ability to become almost invisible and to move silently, the characteristics of a 'burglar'; add to that the adventurous qualities of Bilbo's Tookish blood and he has found just what he's looking for: 'someone to share in an adventure that [he's] arranging' (15). And so it begins: 'something Tookish woke up inside him' (28) and Gandalf has found his burglar; he will also have stirred something Tookish inside the reader and our own desire for adventure will have awoken from its Bagginsish slumber. The marks on the page will have quite disappeared from view, and the vistas of Middle-Earth will open before us.

A great deal of Bilbo's character could be inferred from his home, especially its comforts and familiarities; even more from his physical description. In reading a Shakespeare play we really don't get any of this. Instead we gain knowledge of character solely through people talking. Such as when Romeo's father, Montague, says of him:

> Away from light steals home my heavy son
> And private in his chamber pens himself,
> Shuts up his windows, locks fair daylight out
> And makes himself an artificial night.
>
> (1.1.135–138)

We get a pretty clear picture of a depressed teenager – one familiar to many parents and one that can be recollected by many more young readers. But again, there is something playful, even in the description of Romeo's melancholy, which offers itself to our enjoyment. Take the way 'light', which in this context can only mean illumination, is set against 'heavy' to bring out another latent meaning. And 'heavy', of course, does not refer to weight, but rather to gloom – it is being used metaphorically. In this play words are often pointing away from their ordinary meanings, being enlivened and animated, so even when ambiguity is not to the purpose, Shakespeare's characters wake us up to its possibilities and draw attention to ideas, such as light and dark, that will echo throughout the play.

CONTEXTS OF CLOSE READING: MEETING PEOPLE

In reading plays or novels character emerges, again, only from language. The **semantic context** is crucial as it is the potential meanings of particular words that will shape our characters. As we have seen at first a word like 'hobbit' doesn't have a semantic context, but after a few pages it begins to. We are, indeed, given a general description that could be a dictionary definition: short, hairy-footed, curly-haired, portly, quick-fingered, quick to laugh, and wary. From eight or ten words we are able to create a picture of something that doesn't exist. This works because of our intuitive understanding of what it often considered quite a complex example of figurative language called **synecdoche**, where parts of things stand for wholes. Our experience with how stories work makes us assume, for example, that there is a face beneath the curly hair and a mouth that laughs even though they are not mentioned, and that the feet are attached to the portly body by legs which, again, though unmentioned are imagined to be short. Words like 'wary' work in a similar way to suggest a kind of nervous energy which we set in juxtaposition to portliness. Out of the semantic contexts of more familiar words we can create things that are new. Romeo's description also emerges through **figurative language**. Here it is the semantic context of **metaphor**. Romeo, we assume, is not 'heavy', but rather depressed. Heavy is used metaphorically. But his character emerges, in contrast to this weight, through light word-play (a feature of the play as a whole). What also emerges in these extracts are two of the stories' **thematic contexts**. In *The Hobbit* this is the conflict between the Baggins and the Took, the settled and the unsettled. In *Romeo and Juliet* it's the theme of light and dark which will transform into love and death. As you'll see in Chapter 3, the thematic context becomes more and more important. In most cases it is the thematic context that helps us to judge which aspects of any text are most likely to have value for our close reading.

PLEASURE 3: CREATING A WORLD OF WORDS

What we are starting to see emerge here is one of the key tensions to be explored in this book: the tension between what we can intuitively enjoy and what happens when we slow reading down and begin to analyse our enjoyment by focusing on particular words and quotations – that is, by *close reading*. We need to begin, though, with the way words just work on us. And work, they do: they can create whole worlds. Middle-

Earth is an obvious example. This is the world of *The Hobbit*. It is the world of words that we enter when we allow ourselves to cross Bilbo's threshold. Indeed, the moment we can think that there's a door to enter we are already there. The key point is that it is our response as readers to language – to those marks on the page – that makes this story-world of three, or even four, dimensions, nothing more. We can take the following passage from a short way into Bilbo's journey and think about what it so easily appears to create.

> Then they came to lands where people spoke strangely, and sang songs Bilbo had never heard before. Now they had gone far on into the Lone-Lands, where there were no people left, no inns, and the roads grew steadily worse. Not far ahead were dreary hills, rising higher and higher, dark with trees. On some of them were old castles with an evil look, as if they had been built by wicked people. Everything seemed gloomy, for the weather that day had taken a nasty turn.
>
> (47)

This is one of those descriptive passages where nothing much happens, but it makes several important moves that give depth, breadth and time to Middle-Earth. First, Bilbo leaves his own people (who would speak like him) and customs (who would sing familiar songs) behind. Second, with a rather odd use of an extended 'now', which doesn't quite fit with the sense of change and deterioration given by 'grew steadily worse', they leave 'people' behind altogether and enter the evocatively consonant 'Lone Lands'. Then there is a view ahead of 'dreary hills' whose own history is marked by – and there's a subtle shift to Bilbo's perspective – the 'old castles with an evil look'. We have here a tremendous sense of space left behind, of space in front, of moving through time (Bilbo's and the land's) and of being in the present moment – the *now* in which it is beginning to rain and in which a threat is beginning to grow. This is how story can create worlds, by using language to represent time, space and feeling.

Plays don't usually have storytellers accompanying the action and setting the changing scenes, adding digressions, and offering us comfort. In *Romeo and Juliet* we have seen the Prologue function in this way, but typically in a play things have to happen in more or less real time; or, at least, the time it takes an actor to perform a speech or us to read it. Nonetheless, this can still present to us a kind of world. For example, take a few lines from one of Romeo's more famous speeches: 'But soft, what light through yonder window breaks?/It is the east, and Juliet is the sun!/Arise fair sun and kill the envious moon' (2.2.2–4). One thing to recall about Shakespeare's plays is that they were, by and large, written to have been performed in daylight without the benefits of stage lighting. As such it is the language alone that has to create the darkness – for the audience as much as for a reader. Romeo's words 'But soft, what light through yonder window breaks' may give us the light but they imply the darkness against which that light shines out. Now it's also important that though Romeo appears to be looking toward Juliet's famous balcony (indeed, many viewers or readers of *Romeo and Juliet* are waiting for this scene; this is another of the play's pleasures) she does not enter until *after* this speech; he is looking only toward her window. Actually, he does not even know it is *her* window. The speech, then, is about what he desires, not what he sees. It is also about what we, as readers, desire too. There is no sun (it is eclipsed by the language), no Juliet (she is yet to enter) and no moon (it's 'really' daytime). Romeo's language *creates* these meaningful images and we, though the work of our imaginations, share in his creation.

CONTEXTS OF CLOSE READING: CREATING A WORLD OF WORDS

Attention to the ways words work together to modify each other, that is, their **syntactic context**, can reveal, for example, the way Tolkien uses negations to separate Bilbo from his home: songs he'd 'never' heard', lands with 'no' people and no 'inns'. The syntactic contexts of the nouns create the necessary absence of familiarity – it's a pattern that began in the first description of the hobbit hole – 'not' nasty, dirty, wet or dry. Time, too, can be revealed by analysis of the syntactic context. The 'then' and the 'now' and the 'that day' merge Bilbo's movement through time and space, creating the breadth of the world. In many ways language is generating something out of nothing as there is no more a Middle-Earth than there is a 'moon' in

Romeo's daylit speech. The **syntactic context** in Shakespeare's play, though, is a lot more complex and elliptical. The 'light' that comes from a window becomes, by reference to 'the east', a daybreak and thus Juliet, the desired source of the light, becomes the sun. The sun is then set against the moon, which both figures the real time of day and is meant figuratively to represent virgin femininity (its **semantic context**).

PLEASURE 4: HEARING VOICES

Coming to understand a play almost necessarily creates a rather enjoyable tension between hearing and reading. However, it's not altogether clear quite what we 'hear' when we *read* the play's words, or what we may 'see' when we *hear* them. Rather the language fashions for us a world in which hearing, reading and understanding seem to obey different rules from normal discourse. Take Juliet's reflections on voice at the end of the scene we've just been looking at: 'Hist, Romeo, hist! O, for a falconer's voice/To lure this tassel-gentle back again'. (2.2.158–159) In performance we would hear the rasp of the 'Hist … hist!'; in reading we *hear* nothing. Yet we are still impressed by something in our auditory imagination. The extended falconry metaphor is a bit obscure (a 'tassel-gentle' is a male peregrine falcon – and would we really want Juliet to be as shrill as a huntsman calling for his bird?). The sound of what she is saying is, arguably, less important that the meaning she is trying to get across. But often sounds force themselves onto our attention, even if we are reading. How could we not 'hear' and enjoy the euphony of Romeo's response? 'It is my soul that calls upon my name./How silver-sweet sound lovers' tongues by night,/Like softest music to attending ears' (2.2.163–165). It is clear that, in the play, Romeo 'hears' Juliet (his 'soul'); but when we read we also hear his response; we take account of the patterns and appreciate, for example, the lyricism of all those repeated s/z/t sounds. But what exactly does 'silver-sweet' sound like? It is borrowing the clean and precious shine of silver and the desirable taste of sweetness; both of these metaphors suggest the sound of 'lover's tongues' without offering anything like a concrete description of either his or her voice: nothing we can 'hear'. Indeed, the image uses sight and taste, not hearing. The way that language can work with our senses – sight, taste and hearing, and no doubt touch and smell too (think of Bilbo's 'hole') is clearly one of the reasons it affects us to so strongly. When that is attached to meanings that we can interpret, this pleasure grows exponentially.

CONTEXTS OF CLOSE READING: HEARING VOICES

In close reading we often need to attend to a sound we don't actually hear but somehow must imagine. If a character 'gasps' or there's an exclamation mark after a piece of dialogue, we recognise these emotional markers. This is part of the **syntactic context** where words affect the meaning of other words. In a novel '"Oh," sighed Bilbo' is very different from '"Oh!" gasped Bilbo.' Storytellers, or 'narrators', employ these markers to guide our responses. Another pleasure we get from sound – even in reading – comes from repetition with variation. This is the **iterative context**. A phrase like Romeo's 'How silver-sweet sound lover's tongues by night' gets its beauty in part from the complex metaphor (the **semantic context**), borrowing the clean and precious shine of silver and the desirable taste of sweetness; but also from the iteration of the s/z/t sounds across the line. This creates a kind of compactness and unity that is unerringly effective. We'll be looking at the iterative context in Chapters 5 and 6.

PLEASURE 5: FINDING OURSELVES

Identification is one of the chief pleasures of reading, and Bilbo's character is defined in number of ways that will make him identifiable for Tolkien's expected reader. We've already noted that his hobbit-hole is both strange and familiar. This familiarity extends to Bilbo as we tend, in reading, to associate character with place; it's a common storytelling device, as we shall see further on in this book. It is, though, also important that Bilbo becomes different, for it is in that difference that we may discover unknown aspects of ourselves. And this, of course, is exactly what happens to Bilbo as his adventure progresses: he is taken outside of himself in order to realise his own potential. The first thing that begins the re-casting of Bilbo as a character fit for adventure is the mark that Gandalf puts on his perfectly round, and freshly painted, green door. To the dwarves it immediately means: '*Burglar wants a good job, plenty of Excitement and reasonable Reward*' (32; author's italics). This then becomes a role that Bilbo desires to assume, especially when he overhears the dwarf Gloin's description of him as a 'little fellow bobbing and puffing on the mat [who] looks more like a grocer than a burglar!' (31) That Bilbo wants to live up to being a burglar rather than a grocer is demonstrated at the first opportunity, which is the company's early encounter with the trolls. He has, as the narrator informs us, 'read a good many things he had neither seen nor done'; and as such he knows that 'A really first-class and legendary burglar would at this point have picked the troll's pockets [...] and walked off without their noticing him' (52). Bilbo, like us, enjoys adventure stories. He knows the genre and thus the character he needs to be. Of course, as a first attempt it necessarily goes wrong (Bilbo needs to have room to grow); he and the dwarves are all captured, and Gandalf has to save them.

It is only when Gandalf is handily removed from the tale, at the edge of the dark and forbidding Mirkwood, and at the beginning of 'the most dangerous part of all the journey' (173), that Bilbo can come into his own. In the dark wood Bilbo saves the dwarves from giant spiders and then rescues them from an underground Elven kingdom. Just before Bilbo rescues the dwarves, when he is stuck in the Elven kingdom, invisible and hungry, the narrator reminds us of how far Bilbo feels he is from successfully fulfilling his role: '"I am like a burglar that can't get away, but must go on miserably burgling the same house day after day," he thought. "[...] I wish I was back in my hobbit-hole by my own warm fireside with the lamp shining!"' (214). But once he's worked out his plan and told the dwarves, we see that not only in his eyes, but also in the eyes of the dwarves, he is transformed: 'they all trusted Bilbo. Just what Gandalf had said would happen, you see. Perhaps that was part of his reason for going off and leaving them' (215–216) The narrator's voice comes in here and assures us of Bilbo's progress. And by the time the company get to the dragon's mountain 'he had become the real leader in their adventure' (268). This new Bilbo, the *de facto* leader of a group that contains an exiled king, will walk resolutely into a dragon's den. And though we, as readers, have not necessarily changed in the same way, some small adventurous spark of our own has been nurtured into a light by which we can see analogous aspects of our own potential for growth.

The action of *Romeo and Juliet*, unlike *The Hobbit*, doesn't take place over months, but over just a few days (from one early summer Sunday morning to the following Thursday at dawn). There's isn't a great deal of time for growth and trans-formation – it is not that aspect of these characters that we identify with. Indeed, the pleasure of Romeo and Juliet as *characters* lies somewhere else entirely: namely in their archetypal qualities. They are 'the lovers'; it would hardly befit them, once they've found each other, to get complicated, to have second thoughts, to have divided sensibilities (this would turn the play into a romantic comedy). What we identify with is not, as with Bilbo, his recognisable limitations and his gradual elevation in his own and others' eyes, but rather some kind of ideal sense of what it is to be a lover; and, moreover, to be a *doomed* lover. An example is Romeo's response to his exile from Verona, and thus his forced separation from Juliet, for killing her cousin, Tybalt:

> There is no world without Verona's walls
> But purgatory, torture, hell itself;
> Hence 'banished' is banish'd from the world,
> And world's exile is death. Then 'banished'
> Is death, misterm'd.

(3.3.17–21)

As 'Heaven is here/Where Juliet lives' (3.3.29–30) then all other places are hell. There is no middle ground in the lover's discourse. For Romeo to be 'banished' is not merely to be exiled from Verona, but 'from the world', because it is the same thing to be parted from Juliet as to be dead; and 'banished' is 'death mistermed'; that is, another word for death. He, as a lover, will not listen to any kind of reason from Friar Laurence, who has been his unstinting support, because, as Romeo puts it, 'Thou canst not speak of that thou dost not feel' (3.3.64). Only a lover knows what a lover feels and can speak of it. Both Juliet's and Romeo's characters demonstrate the archetypal nature of the lover: they are beyond reason, just as they should be. And we enjoy having our own understanding and expectations of the world, and perhaps even a version of our own experiences, reflected back to us.

CONTEXT OF CLOSE READING: FINDING OURSELVES

For any character to be identifiable they will usually need to repeat certain behaviours or patterns of speech that are already familiar to us or that we can readily sympathise with. This is the part of the **iterative context** that creates what, in Chapter 6, I shall call a character's **credible continuity**. In Bilbo we get, for example, his repeated longing to be at home, but, moreover, we see a recurrent tension between his Bagginsish reserve and his Tookish sense of adventure, the development of which becomes one of the novel's themes. These poles are, happily, far enough apart that anyone can probably find themselves on the scale and identify with the hobbit. Romeo, like Bilbo, is made up of iterations. These are usually tied to the **thematic context** of the lover. The thematic development here, though, is that this play becomes serious, and ultimately tragic, when the lover's view of the world turns reality into a dark fantasy. This, again, is an identifiable representation of what thwarted love *should* do. What we often follow as we read is an intertwining of the thematic and the iterative contexts that gives the necessary shape to any discernible character growth and to the development of the plot, elements which are themselves central to our ability to relate to the story.

PLEASURE 6: ANTICIPATING PLOTS

In some ways, of course, *The Hobbit*'s plot can be anticipated – its subtitle is 'There and Back Again' after all. But it does, unlike *Romeo and Juliet*, involve the growth and change of its central character. A key moment occurs about a third of the way into the story, when Bilbo becomes lost in dark goblin tunnels and separated from his companions. His first thought is a Baggins thought: 'frying bacon and eggs in his own kitchen' (91); thus it is as a Baggins (and as such 'one of us') that he begins to move off into the labyrinth. But he is comforted by the elven blade he found in the trolls' lair and the weight of history it brought with it: 'It was rather splendid to be wearing a blade made in Gondolin for the goblin-wars of which so many songs had been sung' (92). Deep in the tunnels by an underground lake he encounters a creature called Gollum and they play 'the riddle game'. More through luck than judgement Bilbo wins the contest, but Gollum attempts to deceive him and sneaks to his island in the lake to find his magic ring of invisibility. We know that Bilbo has, apparently inadvertently, discovered this ring. The hobbit hears Gollum's anguished cries when he discovers 'his precious' is lost; but 'Utterly miserable as Gollum sounded, Bilbo could not find much pity in his heart' (106–107) for the vile creature. A little later, though, when Bilbo wearing the ring has invisibly followed Gollum to the exit from the Mountain corridors, he finds the slimy creature blocking his way out:

> Bilbo almost stopped breathing, and went stiff himself. He was desperate. He must get away, out of this horrible darkness, while he had any strength left. He must fight. He must stab this foul thing, put its eyes out, kill it. It meant to kill him. No, not a fair fight. He was invisible now. Gollum had no sword. Gollum had not actually threatened to kill him. Or tried yet. And he was miserable, alone, lost. A sudden understanding, a pity mixed with horror, welled up in Bilbo's heart: a glimpse of endless unmarked days without light or hope of betterment, hard stone, cold fish, sneaking and whispering. All these thoughts passed in a flash of a second. He trembled. And then quite suddenly in another flash, as if lifted by new strength and resolve, he leapt.

> (112)

In reading this we are directly drawn into Bilbo's feelings, physical and emotional. In this passage we see that Bilbo's body acts first and he stops breathing and goes stiff. Then the narrator seems directly to channel Bilbo's thoughts (replace those 'he's and 'him's with 'I's and 'me's and you'll see what I mean: '*I* must fight', 'It meant to kill *me*', etc.) which are violent and frightened, coming in short bursts. At this pivotal moment there is a change of tone. Bilbo's sense of justice wells up: 'No, not a fair fight.' This, again, is not the prose of the narrator, but represents a swift change in Bilbo's thoughts. Suddenly Gollum as 'it' ('kill *it*. *It* meant to kill him') becomes 'Gollum', a named being. As a vulnerable creature 'he' is now worthy of Bilbo's pity and he begins to sympathise with Gollum; to understand his suffering. In the 'flash of a second' Bilbo moves from being a desperate killer to being an understanding sympathiser. None of these thoughts are particularly Bagginsish or Tookish; they are, rather, considered and just. Bilbo has begun to move on; he judges based on the needs of the moment, not on some prejudice of blood. How can we not enjoy and identify with this change of heart, a change that we are unlikely to have anticipated? Our sense of any work's plot will very often be intimately tied to the way its characters develop and change.

The thrust of any plot exerts a pressure on our reading pleasure that can take at least two forms. The plot can, as in the case of *Romeo and Juliet*, be something we know in advance and watch approach. Or it can, as we've just seen with *The Hobbit*, be something less expected, that we learn in our reading. In *Romeo and Juliet*, then, the pressure of the plot's tragic inevitability will colour our reading in advance. Take a short speech by Juliet, as she wakes with Romeo, and hears the dawn lark singing:

> It is the lark that sings so out of tune,
> Straining harsh discords and unpleasing sharps.
> Some say the lark makes sweet division.
> This doth not so, for she divideth us.

> (3.5.27–30)

Our reading of these lines cannot escape the tragic recognition that the lovers must be divided. Juliet herself seems to show some insight into this: the beautiful song of the lark, that sweetens the 'division' between dark and light, night and day, becomes a 'harsh discord' when it symbolises the split between her and Romeo. And, of course, we know that this division will be final and their love is doomed, as

Juliet predicts a few lines later: 'Methinks I see thee, now thou are so low,/As one dead in the bottom of a tomb' (3.5.55–56) Which is exactly where Juliet will next see her Romeo when she awakens at the end of Act 5. This inevitability haunts the play as we anticipate the dark pleasures of tragedy amidst the impossible hopes of their romance. How we understand and enjoy any part of a text will depend on how we understand the whole of it.

CONTEXTS OF CLOSE READING: ANTICIPATING PLOTS

The **generic context** will always be significant when we think about plot. Genres, after all, tend to limit plot possibilities. Tragedies will end badly for our heroes, adventure or fantasy stories will, typically, end well. The generic context guides our expectations. Even so, as you start to think about a text as a *whole,* two different contexts of close reading become increasingly important and more closely related: the **thematic** and the **iterative**. Plot, for example, in a literary text, is inevitably developed through the iterative context, especially as it relates to the events which bring about changes in character. A character, as we will see in Chapter 5, is nothing more than a series of iterations – a name frequently attached (through its **syntactic context**) to behavioural traits. This will, inevitably, feed into the themes which will often both determine and be revealed by those changes. We can see this clearly in both the case of Bilbo and Juliet. What happens, and what is most important for any close reading, is that these larger contexts, the generic, the thematic and the iterative, actually become the contexts that inform the interpretation of the smallest details, right down to the **semantic context**. Thus our reading of the pronouns in the above extract becomes much more significant in the light of the Baggins/Took intertwined iterative and thematic contexts, just as Juliet's generically foreboding lament fits the thematic context of light/dark and love/death.

PLEASURE 7: LESSONS ALONG THE WAY

That Bilbo has grown is one thing, but I'm not sure we'd get as much pleasure out of the book if we weren't at least partially convinced it had had some kind of effect on us too. Many of these effects have already been discussed. We enjoy the characters, the plot, the voices and the language they use. We enjoy the comforts and the perils, the latter all the more because of the promise of the former. We enjoy identifying with the hero: sharing his normality, wondering at his strangeness, sympathising with his choices, watching him mature, seeing the new world of Middle-Earth through his eyes. But is there a different message in the book, some kind of lesson that we take in along with our pleasure? Well, there are some reasonably obvious ones such as 'finding yourself' in your own differences. Bilbo, as you'll remember, starts off being a 'respectable' hobbit whose answer on any question you could tell 'without the bother of asking him' (12). He ends up 'no longer quite respectable [and] held by all the hobbits of the neighbour-hood to be "queer"'; even so, as the narrator tells us, 'he did not mind. He was quite content; and the sound of the kettle on his hearth was ever after more musical than it had been even in the quiet days before the Unexpected Party' (363). This final detail is crucial: not only does the hobbit not care that he has changed and lost his place in the community, this change has actually enriched Bilbo's taste for his former life. He has not just altered, he has *improved*, and his ability to appreciate his world (both the Baggins and the Took side) has grown. Bilbo's adventures are, as such, analogous to an ideal reading experience.

There is another lesson that emerges at the end when Gandalf reminds Bilbo of the other forces that also worked toward his success: 'You don't really suppose, do you, that all your adventures and escapes were managed by mere luck, just for your sole benefit? You are a very fine person, Mr Baggins, and I am very fond of you; but you are only quite a little fellow in a wide world after all!' (365). This introduces, at the very end of the story, a new tension. All along we have wanted to believe that it was Bilbo who was responsible for his choices (*choosing* to be a burglar rather than a grocer, *choosing* to take pity on Gollum), but Gandalf implies that it was not the hobbit but rather Fate that determined the outcome of his adventure. Bilbo's story is just one chapter in the ongoing and fateful unfolding of Middle-Earth's grand narrative, and 'quite a little one' at that.

Fate, though, has a darker side; a message that can be read a little differently. This is the primacy in *The Hobbit* of blood and blood lines; the threads of destiny that run through veins. We see this in the conflict between Bilbo's Baggins and Took ancestry. We see it in Thorin's 'right' to rule; which on his death defers to his cousin, Dain. We see it in Bard, the direct descendent of the last king of Dale, who re-assumes his throne once he has killed the dragon. Destiny is tied to particular behaviours, and also to particular values, such as the 'natural' rights of inherited monarchy. Bilbo's own 'comfortable' existence, however it is reconceived after his adventures, is equally conservative: a rural idyll that belongs to a certain kind of English idealism that is all the more resonant for appearing in a different world. But, of course, Middle-Earth isn't supposed to be a different world. In Tolkien's prefatory remarks we are told that 'This is a story of long ago' (9); it is not a story of an invented land, but of *our own* fictional pre-history. These qualities, then, accrue a kind of quasi-eternal value. That *The Hobbit* was written in the 1930s, at the time when the aristocracy was crumbling and the countryside invaded by industry at a more rapid rate than ever before, should hardly come as a surprise. On the one hand, then, the story is an escape from that world. On the other it is a revelation of what, according to the tale's underlying message, ought to be that world's deepest values.

And what of *Romeo and Juliet*? Beyond its beautiful poetry and representation of archetypal love, and in addition to its variation on a well-known story and its play of language, what does it offer us? Perhaps surprisingly it's not dissimilar to *The Hobbit*; or, at least, there are significant parallels. Certainly, Fate is there from the off – the prologue tells us the end, and, really, we already knew it. It would be hard, though, to say it was the cosmic fate of *The Hobbit*, despite the poeticism of the 'star-crossed' lovers. It is rather a fate that is *human*. Tragedy is brought about by human failings. It is also a fate that is generalisable. Yes, this is a few days in Verona hundreds of years ago; but it is also every lover, everywhere. As with *The Hobbit*, blood is also central. The whole drama hangs on a blood feud: the medieval idea that family honour is more important than community or, indeed, individuality. But rather than, as in *The Hobbit*, the dynamics of blood working themselves out in a single character, it is divided between the two lovers and then extended to their families. And in contrast to Bilbo's 'Baggins' and 'Took' sides, the Montagues and the Capulets are merely mirrors of each other; there is nothing distinctive about either of them. And, of course, that is the point – they are feuding over nothing, or at least, nothing that the life of the play reveals. Here, in the end, it is not community or individuality that triumphs. Far from it; though the Montagues and the Capulets agree to settle their differences, it is the Prince, who has the last word:

> Go hence to have more talk of these sad things.
> Some will be pardoned and some punished,
> For never was a story of more woe
> Than this of Juliet and her Romeo.
>
> (5.3.306–309)

It is up to the aristocracy to restore order; though in Verona that can only be done with the will of the families, who had ignored the Prince prior to the tragedy of their mutual loss. Both works, then, have a similar faith in feudal power structures, even though their interest is in the lives of individuals who are, in many ways, both typical and archetypal. They are about how ordinary small things fit into larger, often implicit, structures. We always need to be wary about such structures, as the final parts of this book will explore.

CONTEXTS OF CLOSE READING: LESSONS ALONG THE WAY

While it might be kindest to the authors of these works to take the lessons we learn as the ultimate consequence of the **thematic contexts** of their works and as something intended, unfortunately it's rarely that simple. Texts are not hermetically sealed objects and are certainly not things that must be taken entirely on their own terms. Rather they provoke perhaps unintended, even **adversarial**, questions – does Tolkien really mean to promote a monarchical rural culture based on bloodlines and inheritance or does he really mean to say that the world can be improved when small people do the right thing? If so how would these potentially conflicting political messages affect any young reader of the text? Similarly, does Shakespeare's own political ending to his tragedy reflect life in an imagined medieval Verona or rather a Renaissance England where the tensions between established hierarchical structures and emergent individuals have become critical? Texts have a wider range of contexts, which here I am calling **adversarial contexts**, which engage with these kinds of questions. These adversarial contexts might include historicist readings that locate texts against their contemporary backdrops, they might include Marxist readings which would ask searching questions about a text's political structures. As we shall see in Chapter 7, the questions posed by feminists, psychoanalysts, ecocritics and literary theorists of many a stripe can each become new contexts for close reading, transforming any, and maybe all, of the contexts that have been introduced so far.

AND ONE MORE PLEASURE: RE-READING

At the beginning of this chapter I noted a few things about reading that give pleasure: escape, new experiences, new people, the encounter with brilliant language, coming to new understandings, being caught up in a plot, and re-reading to possess a book entirely. The only one of these I haven't covered so far is re-reading. There's no doubt that books like *The Hobbit* and plays like *Romeo and Juliet* can be enjoyed, in a transitory fashion, in just one read. But, as the word *transitory* suggests, such pleasures are brief – they are not firm possessions. Doubtless as a reader you have often gained the most pleasure from the books you have read and re-read until you felt that you almost owned them: when you got to the point where you could argue about them with friends; could recall plot details and lines of text; felt like you knew what each character looked like and could hear how they sounded. In many respects re-reading is the *only* truly valuable reading, and certainly the only one that works for *close* reading. It is only when we are apprised of how a piece of writing works as a whole that we are able to understand each of its individual elements, such as words, sentences, paragraphs, stanzas, scenes, chapters, character, plot, themes, etc. We may be able to hold a very basic narrative in our heads after just one read, but usually we need to revisit a story, often several times, to be able to grasp it as a whole. Moving, as we must, from part to whole and then from whole to part, in a kind of upward spiral, our understanding and our reading pleasure increase with that spiral's upward trajectory. This is the *enjoyment* of a narrative in both of that word's senses: to take pleasure from something, but also to *possess* it. This is what you, as a student of literature, will gain from engaging with this book.

2

THE SEMANTIC CONTEXT

That words have meanings is something everybody knows. That most words *usually* have, and all words can *potentially* have, more than one meaning is something that we also rely on to be able to communicate effectively. A particular word's **semantic context** is the range of possible meanings that any such word may reasonably be said to have. Just what is reasonable is something that much literary language tends to stretch, and the more there is going on in a word the more there is to enjoy. Nevertheless, there are usually limits to any word's semantic context. In what follows I offer three main ways of thinking about these limits: the *situation* in which the word is used, the *history* of that word and the extent to which the word is meant to be – or can be taken as – *figurative*.

1 SITUATIONAL SEMANTICS

It's a pretty good start when close reading to recognise that books are made up of words. It seems obvious, but strangely we tend to think of books as made up of characters, voices, places, colours, sounds, feelings, and so on – as we saw with *The Hobbit* and *Romeo and Juliet* in the first chapter. Actually it's not surprising at all that we don't think of books as made up of words. After all the purpose of a word, as of any sign or symbol, is to indicate or point to something else. Therefore, when good readers read they don't pay too much attention to the language but rather to what is being described as it takes some kind of shape in their minds. The words become transparent. However – and this, arguably, is one of the things that defines 'literature' – literary language tends to be interested in words as things in their own right. Words are not, then, transparent, but are part of what is interesting about a book, a poem or a play. For the close reader, language needs to become opaque in important ways such that visibility is returned to it. Gandalf has, as noted above, already made the reader aware of the lack of transparency of words when he calls Bilbo to account for wishing him a 'good morning': '"What do you mean?" he said. "Do you wish me a good morning, or mean that it is a good morning whether I want it or not; or that you feel good this morning; or that it is a morning to be good on?"' (15). This is language drawing attention to itself; to what I am calling its 'semantic context'. When Bilbo says 'good morning' he is unlikely *to be taken* to mean anything contained by those words, it's merely a formula of politeness. As soon as the words' potential meanings are analysed, as Gandalf does, the phrase becomes hopelessly ambiguous for everyday use. It's as if all those meanings for 'word' outlined in the introduction were at work at once.

However, we know the correct (or the most likely) meaning from the *situation* – a meeting of two people before noon. This is the setting which gives the words their semantic context. 'Good morning', then, is normally a way of saying 'hello'; a more or less casual greeting. This has been recognised by Bilbo, and also by the reader. It is something of a surprise when Gandalf refuses to join in with the convention. Even so, if the situation changes, the meaning of an expression changes. When Bilbo next uses the phrase 'good morning', after Gandalf has invited him on an adventure, an idea the hobbit rejects, it has quite a different meaning:

> 'Good morning!' he said at last. 'We don't want any adventures here, thank you! You might try over The Hill or across The Water.' By this he meant that the conversation was at an end.
> 'What a lot of things you do use *Good morning* for!' said Gandalf. 'Now you mean you want to get rid of me, and that it won't be good till I move off.'
>
> (16)

Gandalf is offering a semantic analysis of Bilbo's words and in analysing them he is, like an effective literary critic, refusing to allow their obvious meaning, given the context, to stand or to remain unspoken: 'good morning' as 'goodbye'. And that is because he wants to change the context. He doesn't want a polite meeting between people who understand each other and for whom 'good morning' is a flexible formula signifying both 'hello' and 'goodbye'. Gandalf wants to excite uncertainty, to unsettle Bilbo and awaken his Tookish spirit from its Bagginsish slumbers. To this end he undermines Bilbo's banal phrase. The point, though, for us as interpreters is to recognise that the meaning of 'good morning', its productive semantic content, is entirely dependent on its situational context. This is a generalisable principle. *All* meaning is determined by context.

2 HISTORICAL SEMANTICS

History is important because the meanings of words change over time. Shakespeare's writing is a familiar object lesson in this regard that everyone has probably had to wrestle with. In the Prologue to *Romeo and Juliet* we get the phrase 'the two hours' traffic of our stage' (1.0.12). All of these words are familiar in the twenty-first century, but it's still an odd expression to contemporary ears. The word that needs semantic contextualisation is 'traffic'. For the last few generations this word has predominantly meant the movement of vehicles along a road (free flowing *traffic* or *traffic* jams) or the movement of, often illicit, goods (she *trafficked* stolen items). This suggests, perhaps, that the play will 'move across' the stage for two hours. This might work and be a useful way of thinking about the word. But it might also be worth thinking about what this word, traffic, meant in the 1590s. When we look in the *Oxford English Dictionary* we find that using traffic to refer to moving vehicles was first recorded in 1825, so it's unlikely to be relevant to the 1590s. In that time the word did have its trading connotations, but it also, by extension, meant 'business' or even 'communication' – meanings that died out in the nineteenth century. These meanings seem much more likely for the Prologue than either trade or transport – e.g. 'the two hours' [business] of our stage'. Time, then, or the historical sense of how words work, is a key element of any given word's semantic context and will help us to understand the likely meaning of any given phrase.

Without doubt the most useful tool in the close reader's arsenal when thinking about the semantic context is the *Oxford English Dictionary* (*OED*). What the *OED* gives you is not just the meaning of a word, but also how any given word's meaning has shifted over time. Additionally it provides the origin of the word (where known), which can be useful as writers tend to know and exploit these things (as we'll see in a moment). It's not always the case, as with 'traffic', that we need to disentangle contemporary meanings from historic ones. Sometimes words have fallen into disuse and sometimes they can be ambiguous. *Romeo and Juliet* provides useful examples in both cases. Let's look more fully at a few words in Romeo's 'But soft, what light through yonder window' speech that we looked at in the last chapter, giving them their immediate context:

> But soft, what light through yonder window breaks?
> It is the east, and Juliet is the sun!
> Arise, fair sun, and kill the envious moon
> Who is already sick and pale with grief
> That thou her maid art far more fair than she.
> Be not her maid since she is envious,
> Her vestal livery is but sick and green
> And none but fools do wear it. Cast it off.
>
> (2.2.2–9)

Here, when Romeo refers to Juliet's 'vestal livery' we are unlikely to know to what he is referring. 'Livery', for example, is a word that is no longer in common usage – it means a distinctive dress or uniform, usually worn by a noble's serving men. As such, Juliet is figured as a servant of the moon; she, metaphorically, wears its 'livery'. If we check in the *OED* the word actually has over a dozen entries but none of them is more compelling. Livery is, however, modified by 'vestal', a stranger word and even less in common usage. The *OED* gives six meanings:

A. ADJECTIVE

1   Vestal virgin n. one of the priestesses (originally four, subsequently six in number) who had charge of the sacred fire in the temple of Vesta at Rome. (1475–1891).

2   Of fire, etc.: Of or pertaining to Vesta. (1599–1853).
3   Resembling a priestess of Vesta in respect of chastity; chaste, pure, virgin. (1595–1818).
4   Pertaining to, characteristic of, a vestal virgin or virgins; marked by chastity or purity. (1594–1847).

B. NOUN

1   A vestal virgin. (1579–1828).
2   A virgin; a chaste woman; a nun. (1593–1847).

After each meaning the *OED* gives a series of quotations. These quotations give the date range in which we have evidence that the word was used in writing, e.g., for B1: '1579 T. North tr. *Plutarch Liues* 73 He also hath the keeping of the holy virgines which they call Vestales'. I have put these dates in brackets after the above definitions. What is interesting here is that a lot of these meanings came into usage about the same time as *Romeo and Juliet* was composed in the late 1590s (A2, A3, A4, B1, B2). This suggests that Shakespeare would have been part of a world in which these definitions were *all* possible. So which is most likely? In Romeo's speech the word is being used as an adjective, so we can discount the B meanings; or at least relegate them to less likely connotations, as they are nouns. So we have A1–4. Now, 1, 3 and 4 seem to mean much the same thing in referring to the priestesses of Vesta, who are remarkable for their virginity, chastity and purity. But each of these meanings is also registering a subtle change of meaning. We start with the word meaning the actual priestess (A1), then it comes to mean 'resembling' the priestess (A3), then it comes to mean pertaining to the qualities of such a priestess (A4). The other meaning, A2, is of fire or the god Vesta (as in *Swan Vesta* matches). If we feed these back into Romeo's speech, what do we get?

1   Juliet's livery is that of a vestal virgin;
2   Juliet's livery is flaming;
3   Juliet's livery resembles a priestess;
4   Juliet's livery is marked by chastity and purity.

In this context 1, 2 and 3 are extremely unlikely (the idea of Juliet on fire does fit in with her as the sun, but at this moment Romeo is associating her with the moon). Which leaves us with 4 – Juliet's livery, as a servant of the moon, is marked by chastity, virginity, purity. A closer look at the *OED* confirms this, as one of the quotations used for this definition is: '1597 Shakespeare *Romeo & Juliet* ii. i. 50 Her vestall liuerie is but pale and greene'. Shakespeare, usually maintaining the original spelling, is cited in the *OED* more than any other single author. Here the *OED* has helped us to unlock the semantic context of the obscure word 'vestal'. That is, it has given us a potential range of meanings from which we can choose *not* the right one, as though there was only one right way of reading the speech, but the most *productive* ones. What we are interested in getting from the semantic context, then, is the meanings of words that will open up the fullest range of reasonable interpretations for you as a reader to enjoy.

COMPLEXITY CASE STUDY

There are other words which when considered in terms of their wider meanings can open up some of the language in *Romeo and Juliet*. For example, the word 'die' is used many times in the play, but this leads to an unexpected ambiguity. The 'Prologue' to Act 2 is promising here:

> Now old desire doth in his deathbed lie
> And young affection gapes to be his heir;
> That fair for which love groan'd for and would die,
> With tender Juliet match'd, is now not fair.

> (2.0.1–4)

The basic meaning here is that Romeo's love for Rosaline has waned and his new love for Juliet has waxed, and as such Rosaline's beauty has faded when compared to Juliet's. Line 2.0.3 runs as follows: 'That fair for which love groan'd for and would die'; that is, Romeo would have died for Rosaline's love. This is certainly the most likely meaning, as in the *OED* 'die' has twelve definitions, often with several subsections and almost all of them mean an end to life or a similar diminishment. But meaning 7d is 'To experience a sexual orgasm. (Most common as a poetical metaphor in the late 16th and 17th cent.)' Surely in the context of 'groan' this secondary meaning is plausible, and probably deliberate. Later in the same act we get: 'These violent delights have violent ends/And in their triumph die, like fire and powder/Which, as they kiss, consume'. (2.6.9–11). In Act 3 Juliet says: 'Give me my Romeo; and when I shall die/Take him and cut him out in little stars' (3.2.21–22). Both these contexts allow for two different meanings of 'die' to be reasonably sustained, and, indeed, probably intended. Ambiguity is, in each of these cases, productive. Indeed, the relationship between 'to die' as a tragic end and 'to die' as a romantic consummation is surely at the very heart of a play like *Romeo and Juliet*. Understanding this also lies at the heart of our potential to enjoy fully what the words put before us.

3 FIGURATIVE SEMANTICS

Now, I noted above that words usually point to something else; that is, words are not the things they describe. This is self-evident and also for the most part not much of a problem as all we need to do is put together the image of what the words describe as we read – so Bilbo's round green door with its shiny knob doesn't present any real problems, even though the word 'green' is not green and the word 'round' is not round. It's likely that each reader will imagine a different shade of green and a different shaped knob – if they really set to picturing the scene – but that is to be expected. At least the words conform to what they are describing and we don't see the words but the image – the door is not, for example, symbolic of something else. As such these words can be taken 'literally' in terms of their world-creating powers.

However, all too often in literary works words don't literally mean what they say. Words are used figuratively (as with 'livery' and 'vestal' above). The understanding of the way figurative language works is one of the most important elements of literary analysis – and undoubtedly one which provides amongst the keenest rewards. There are a variety of ways in which language can be figurative, but perhaps the most useful to grasp fully are **metaphor, metonymy,**

simile and **synecdoche**. Metaphor and simile are probably pretty familiar, but they can get quite complex, and it's worth having a method to work out their nuances. The other two I'll come onto shortly.

APPRECIATING METAPHOR

Sometimes we come across a piece of really rather ordinary language in a book – and I'll stay with *The Hobbit* for now – that goes like this: 'The dark filled all the room, and the fire died down, and the shadows were lost' (26). In terms of its atmospheric effect this passage works immediately and simply: our trained intuition grasps the sense. But the language is actually quite complex. Can darkness 'fill' a room? Can a fire 'die'? Can shadows become 'lost'? In the first instance the word 'fill', here used as a verb, creates a sense of gradual darkening; it borrows on the connotations of, say, a bottle filling with water, where the content works its way out to the shape of the container. In the second case, the idea of a dying fire is also impossible – as a fire is never alive. But a fire when burning has the animation of something alive: it moves, it has heat; as such it can appear to 'die' when it cools. As the dark fills the room and the fire dies the shadows are lost. Again, shadows cannot become lost – in the literal sense of unable to find their way or being misplaced. Rather the shadows become one with the darkness of the room and we are unable to see them as individual shadows: they are lost to our sight, but they are still there.

In each case here, *filled, died* and *lost*, a metaphor has been used and it shows that even in our most prosaic way of speaking (this can hardly be called poetry, for all its swift effectiveness) we work through metaphors. In a way we can say that this sentence works and is fully intelligible even though it says absolutely nothing that is literally the case. I. A. Richards, mentioned above as a pioneer of close reading, provided a useful model for analysing metaphors. He split the way they work into three parts. In the case of 'the dark filled the room' this would look as follows. First he thought about *what was being described* and called it the **tenor** (in this case, increasing darkness); then he thought about *the actual word* used and called this the **vehicle** (in this case, filled); and then he thought about *what they had in common*, which he called the

ground (in this case, both are taking over a given space). The metaphor is *all three* of these things understood together. What actually happens in most metaphors is that there's something that's very hard to describe, define or conceptualise simply and efficiently (this is the *tenor*) and so another expression that is easier to understand is borrowed (this is the *vehicle*). Because this process is so fundamental to language we often quickly see the connection between them (this connection is the *ground*). So, far from making things more complicated, metaphor in everyday language is usually a way of making things easier to understand.

For the second and third metaphors in the extract this distinction works as shown in Figure 2.1. In each case, a rather complicated thing to express neatly, such as just what happens when a fire loses its intensity, is figured by a much easier concept, in this case *dying* which, because of its familiarity, brings with the required gradual loss of intensity. Similarly, to say something is *lost* is a much simpler and more effective way of saying something is no longer able to be seen, especially as shadows are extremely hard to conceptualise at the best of times – are they still there or not? Richards' idea of tenor, vehicle and ground, then, works with our conventional 'dead' metaphors. As we shall see next, it's even more effective when we are dealing with trickier 'literary' metaphors. Don't worry if you don't quite get the complexities of this method now – you'll be coming across it again at numerous points in what follows, and you'll soon pick it up.

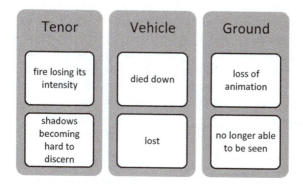

Figure 2.1

LIVING METAPHORS

Dead metaphors can be brought back to life. The early twentieth-century American author F. Scott Fitzgerald was a master of this. Let's take a close slow look at how his narrator in *The Great Gatsby* describes the home of Tom and Daisy Buchanan:

> Their house was even more elaborate than I expected, a cheerful red-and-white Georgian Colonial mansion, overlooking the bay. The lawn started at the beach and ran towards the front door for a quarter of a mile, jumping over sundials and brick walls and burning gardens – finally when it reached the house drifting up the side in bright vines as though from the momentum of its run.
>
> (11–12)

There are a number of more or less dead metaphors here: 'cheerful', 'overlooking' the running and 'jumping' and 'drifting' 'lawn', as well as the 'burning' garden. The one I want to concentrate on is the description of the lawn, which in this case is the *tenor*, and its variety of *vehicles*: running, jumping and drifting. That a lawn 'ran down to the beach' or 'ran up from a beach' is a dead metaphor. It means that it extends just that far. But what Fitzgerald does by having it running and jumping and finally drifting, is rethink the *ground* of that metaphor. This development of the ground reintroduces the movement implicit in 'run' but which is usually lost. Suddenly as a reader we are swept along by the description, following its path over sundials (more than one!), brick walls and the burning gardens; and when we get to the house, normally the end of the run, we are carried up the side of the building as the lawn turns into 'bright vines'. Everything is moving and changing and the figurative language, the play of the re-animated ground, creates that vitality and speed. It's a pleasurable rush not only to be carried across this space, but also to have our everyday language awoken by the skilful use of metaphor. This revival of language is one of the functions of literary writing; enjoying it one of the pleasures of the critical reader.

EXTENDED METAPHORS

Tenor, vehicle and ground, then, are useful ways of analysing how metaphors work, literally taking them apart so that we can reconstruct our knowledge of them with a fuller sense of their function in our pleasure. A metaphor, though, can be even more extended than that used by Fitzgerald. The following example, where Romeo has just come face to face with Juliet, takes it almost as far as it can go:

> Rom: If I profane with my unworthiest hand
>   This holy shrine, the gentle sin is this:
>   My lips, two blushing pilgrims, ready stand
>   To smooth that rough touch with a tender kiss.
> Jul: Good pilgrim, you do wrong your hand too much,
>   Which mannerly devotion shows in this;
>   For saints have hands that pilgrims' hands do touch,
>   And palm to palm is holy palmers' kiss.
> Rom: Have not saints lips, and holy palmers too?
> Jul: Ay, pilgrim, lips that they must use in prayer.
> Rom: O then, dear saint, let lips do what hands do:
>   They pray: grant thou, lest faith turn to despair.
> Jul: Saints do not move, though grant for prayer's sake.
> Rom: Then move not while my prayer's effect I take.
> [*He kisses her*]

(1.5.92–105)

What matters for our purposes here is the extended religious imagery of the pilgrim (Romeo) and the saint's shrine (Juliet), which, as is typical in this play, is ironically turned against itself so religious language is used to discuss burgeoning sexual desire. This is sustained through the push and pull of an increasingly intertwined dialogue, where each fully grasps the swift imagery of the other and makes them serve their purpose, drawing them out. Romeo is more forward in the first four lines, pushing for the kiss; Juliet's rebuff in the next four lines is gentle, and moves from the lips to the hand. Romeo persists with the lips; Juliet turns the mouth into an organ of prayer. Romeo turns that prayer into a kiss, which is granted, at last, by Juliet in her words and in her stillness. We can put this more clearly, and more analytically, into Richards' terms and, by understanding our enjoyment, increase its intensity.

Here the *tenor* of the main metaphor is Juliet, the *vehicle* is 'holy shrine' and the *ground* is the sense of sacredness or adoration that Romeo feels for Juliet. Working out this basic structure is important, but what really matters is being able to point out what work is done by the ground. This ground tells us more about Romeo's feelings than it does about Juliet (at least at this point); but, moreover, it tells us about the way a lover feels about the beloved, which is why we instantly recognise its meaning; that is, the beloved is sacred. That said, the metaphor in its context is not quite that simple as it becomes intertwined with several others. A second metaphor, 'My lips, two blushing pilgrims', works as follows: the *tenor* is Romeo's lips, the *vehicle* is the pilgrim and the *ground* only makes sense if we understand the first metaphor. As Juliet is a sacred site and pilgrims are those who travel to sacred sites, the *ground* is the movement of Romeo's lips towards Juliet as a sacred site. But even this metaphor is itself embedded in a third one of profanation and sin – that is despoiling the sacred site that is Juliet with the touch of Romeo's hand. Here the *tenor* is the touch, the *vehicle* is sin/profanation and the *ground* again only works because Juliet is seen as sacred; someone of whom Romeo is not worthy. Now the lips, as a fourth metaphor, become a pilgrimage to 'smooth' the 'rough touch' of Romeo's unworthy 'profane' hand. The *ground* here is the fact that a pilgrimage is often used to expiate a sin. The complexity of these four intertwined metaphors can be tabulated as shown in Figure 2.2.

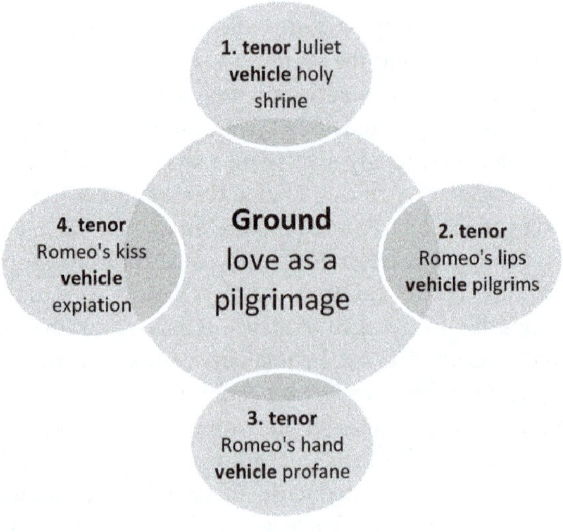

Figure 2.2

It is a very complex and convoluted set of interrelated metaphors that dance before our eyes on the page and take quite a bit of analysis, however easily we may interpret them intuitively. The point, though, is the *way* that each of these words works. They don't work because they indicate one thing – like the green of Bilbo's door (however fuzzily this may be construed by the individual reader) – but because they generate meanings from the various interconnected connotations of their shared ground.

COMPLEXITY CASE STUDY

A potential problem in this respect is demonstrated by Gertrude Stein's statement, from her avant-garde poem 'Sacred Emily' (1922), that 'Rose is a rose is a rose is a rose' (187). On the one hand this couldn't be any more emphatic: someone called Rose *is* a rose. But the very attempt to be clear here creates problems. A person named Rose can't *be* a rose – so what is the meaning of the line? Or is it the purpose of the line to point to the very problem of metaphor – namely that there are always a variety of potential *grounds* at work and if, as in this case, there isn't sufficient context to tame that variety just what Rose is will remain open: she could be beautiful, could smell sweet, could be a lover, could be some kind of ideal, etc. Could each repetition of 'is a rose' point to a different meaning of rose, or re-emphasise just one? The only thing she *can't* be is 'a rose'. So what we are left with is undecidability. What this tells us is precisely how language works by *not* playing the game; that is, in refusing to provide sufficient context Stein's line reminds us that only context can settle meaning into any controllable shape. Poets, of course, along with other writers may choose deliberately to create contexts which allow for the possibility of more than one meaning. A point I'll return to below.

APPRECIATING SIMILE

Metaphor is, perhaps, the principal figurative form, but its close cousin simile is also very common. A popular example is given us by Robert Burns: 'O my luve's like a red, red rose/That's newly sprung in June'. Similes are different from metaphors in that they make a point of directly comparing tenor and vehicle, using 'like', 'as' or something similar, rather than just assuming the relationship. Here the tenor is his love and the vehicle is the red rose. And the ground? Well, in what ways is a rose *like* love? The range of connotations, as with the Stein example, is extremely varied: it's beautiful, it's delicate, it's fresh and 'newly sprung', it grows between thorns, etc. It also has the cultural resonance of a long association with love going back at least until the classical period of ancient Greece. Any of these – or all of them – could be relevant. But there is a further semantic complexity here, which is that the *tenor* itself is uncertain – it could be the speaker of the poem's *feeling* of love or it could be the *person* the speaker is in love with that is like a 'rose'. At that point in the line where the word 'rose' occurs we have a significant point of ambiguity as all of these resonances are at work together and none of them trump the others sufficiently. We also know nothing about the lovers. They may be young, as their love seems to be; but would the meaning actually be more forceful if they were older, but their love still young? There is not enough context to settle the ambiguity – something that the poet, presumably, desired his reader to understand and enjoy.

APPRECIATING METONYMY AND SYNECDOCHE

Metonymy and synecdoche work in a different way from metaphor and simile. They are, arguably, more common in prose – indeed, as we shall see, without metonymy and synecdoche prose really couldn't work at all. What each of these figures does is use a part to represent a whole. For example, to return to *The Great Gatsby*, here's a description of Tom Buchanan, with the key metonymies in bold and synecdoches in italics:

> He had changed since his **New Haven** years. Now he was a sturdy *straw-haired* man of thirty, with a rather *hard mouth* and a supercilious manner. *Two shining arrogant eyes* had established dominance over his face and gave him the appearance of always leaning aggressively forward. Not even the effeminate swank of his **riding clothes** could hide the enormous power of that body – he seemed to fill those **glistening**

boots until he strained the top lacing, and you could see a *great pack of muscle shifting when his shoulder moved* under his thin coat. It was a body capable of enormous leverage – a *cruel body*.

(12)

Metonymy works through association. If you referred, for example, to 'a White House spokesman', where the 'White House' stands for the 'President of the United States of America', you would be using metonymy. When used in literary prose, metonyms can be a very effective shorthand – a way of building up character through associations. Taking a close look at the extract, 'New Haven' is a metonym for Yale University. This reference to the prestigious Northeastern American college immediately locates Tom's social class and his educational background. This is echoed by his riding clothes as, again, we will associate a very particular class with riding. 'Glistening boots' are a slightly different thing. Metonymically they indicate the quality and polish of his outfit – i.e., shiny boots suggest that everything else he wears is well-tailored and of a high standard, and that he has servants to keep that shine. But shiny boots also have another set of connotations: something militaristic (not yet fascistic as that 'Jack boot' association won't be set up until the 1930s, nor yet fetishistic, as that will come later again in the twentieth century). In each case the semantic context of the metonymy is culturally suggestive beyond the literal meaning of the words.

Synecdoche works in a similar way. If you were to say 'all hands on deck' the 'hand' would stand for the whole person. In the extract from *Gatsby*, Tom's physical whole is suggested by a few synecdoches: his 'hard mouth', his 'shining arrogant eyes', and the 'great pack of muscle' of his shoulder. Our assumption as readers is that this isn't all there is of him – a few fragments floating in space. Rather we create the whole of Tom from these few pointers, filling in the rest according to those hints – as we did with Bilbo in Chapter 1. But, moreover, we will create his personality too: hard, arrogant and threateningly strong. This culminates in his 'cruel body', where the physical threat of that body is a synecdoche for the whole person – body and mind; and, through a much wider metonymic association, a whole class.

As it would be quite impossible for any author, no matter how hard they tried, to entirely describe the way a person looks let alone their complete personality, authors use metonymies and synecdoches to enable them to suggest completion. As readers we are very adept at creating the wholes from these parts.

The power of synecdoche and metonymy lies precisely in the potential richness of their semantic context, which allows the novelist to create a vivid world from just a few well-chosen words. The reader will evoke the rest and the picture will be complete. This evocation, this creative act on the reader's part, is another of the chief pleasures – it is why no two reading experiences are quite the same, and equally, why *every* responsive reading experience is valuable.

SUMMARY: THE SEMANTIC CONTEXT

Individual words, then, don't have meanings when they are on their own. This is certainly counterintuitive, as we tend to think that meaning happens when we pile up a certain number of just these individual words. Actually, on the contrary, in the literary texts we have been exploring meaning *only* occurs when there is a pile of sufficient size to create a context for each individual word to do its work. The meaning of a word, its **semantic context**, is not what it has on its own, but those aspects of its potential meaning that are activated when it is put next to other words. We'll look at this in more detail in the next chapter when we look at the **syntactic context**. But even to know what work any particular word can do we need to know some things about that word. We need to know its *situational* setting, i.e. where, when, and by whom it's being spoken. We need to understand its *historical* setting, so that we can get the range of its likely meanings at the moment of utterance. And we need to work out whether it is *literal* or *figurative*, and if figurative just how it is working to point beyond itself. Only then can we begin to work out what meanings are most likely and to what extent the word's semantic context allows room for ambiguity. All these aspects of meaning, then, necessarily work together, and understanding the ways that they work can empower a reader and allow his or her full creativity to begin to emerge.

FURTHER READING

Cleanth Brooks. *The Well Wrought Urn: Studies in the Structure of Poetry*. London: Methuen, 1968

Denis Donoghue. *Metaphor*. Cambridge MA: Harvard University Press, 2014.

William Empson. *Seven Types of Ambiguity*. London: Penguin, 1961.

George Lakoff and Mark Turner. *More than Cool Reason: A Field Guide to Poetic Metaphor*. Chicago: University of Chicago Press, 1989.

I. A. Richards. *The Philosophy of Rhetoric*. Oxford: Oxford University Press, 1936.

3

THE SYNTACTIC AND THEMATIC CONTEXTS

What I hope you are beginning to get the sense of is the ways that the words affect each other to create meaning. Words are the life-giving contexts for other words. Without this context nothing happens. With it *everything* in literature happens. To be able to enjoy the process by which it happens, then, is clearly important. To follow the next steps of the process we need to move up from individual words whose meanings are created by their semantic context and start to think about slightly larger structures. What I shall call here the **syntactic context** – that is, the way words' meanings create literary effects by being *put together in a particular order*, in say, sentences, paragraphs and stanzas. Syntax derives from a Greek word, *syntaxis*, which means just that: an 'orderly or systematic arrangement' (*OED*). In this case then every word in any given extract is a crucial part of the context for all the other words. To a certain extent we've already seen this, as the semantic context of any word can only be determined when we work out its relationship with others. Hitherto, though, the focus has been on liberating the meanings of individual words and deciding on, for example, whether they were figurative or literal or whether a particular historical connotation was relevant. In this section, this shall be broadened to think about how words work in sentences and paragraphs, lines and stanzas.

As we begin to increase the scale of our analysis up to, say, whole poems, then we also need to begin to consider another context. This is the **thematic context**. This is because literary texts are, more often than not, explorations of particular ideas.

We've seen this, for example, in looking at the way *The Hobbit* reflects upon the way Bilbo outgrows both his Tookish and Bagginsish heritage and *Romeo and Juliet* works through the theme of the love and death. This helps us to understand, for example, the ways that certain metaphors work and enable us to think about the text as a whole. The individual words, as they come together, create ideas in the mind of the reader and these ideas develop and change across even quite short works. A work's themes introduce us to new ways of thinking and enlarge our intellectual and emotional capacities. As identified at the outset, this can be one of the most important and enjoyable aspects of reading. Often in reading we have a more or less loose sense of a particular work's ideas and it is often the progression of these ideas that moves us. In this section I want to begin to outline how we can use a work's syntactic and thematic contexts to draw it together as a whole and, equally importantly, use these themes better to understand each of its parts. It is, as with all good close reading, a mutually informative cyclical experience.

1 THE SENTENCE

To begin this scaling up process we can look at a sentence from *The Hobbit*: 'There he lay, a vast red-golden dragon, fast asleep; a thrumming came from his jaws and nostrils, and wisps of smoke, but his fires were low in slumber.' (261) This is actually rather a complex sentence. It's split into two parts by the semi-colon and each half is further divided by commas. In reading we are usually, if we are competent readers, quite unconscious of grammatical structure; but in reflecting on the sentence in order to get the most out of it, it's worth considering how this structure works. Here I'm going to break it down clause by clause and treat it, almost, as if these parts of the sentence were a poem's lines.

> There he lay,
> a vast red-golden dragon,
> fast asleep;
> a thrumming came from his jaws and nostrils,
> and wisps of smoke,
> but his fires were low in slumber.

The first clause runs 'There he lay'. Now, if we bracket this from its immediate situation, all of these words are pretty much meaningless. 'There', without us knowing that the scene takes place in a hall deep in The Lonely Mountain, doesn't function. Similarly, 'he', if we don't know to whom it refers, is empty. Both of these words necessarily point to other words and will only take their meaning from them. 'Lay' at least has a semantic context, mostly likely it is 'to be supine' (as the gender of the unknown thing rules out a chicken, which may also 'lay'), but if we don't know what manner of thing we are dealing with it still won't conjure much of an image.

The next clause, 'a vast red-golden dragon' will no doubt evoke some kind of picture in the reader's mind, and the words 'he' and 'lay' from the earlier clause now begin to function more fully. Indeed, this second clause, containing as it does adjectives (vast, red-golden) and a noun (dragon) is much more straightforwardly meaningful. However, though we begin to get the picture it's important to be aware that these words only work because they are terrifically, and necessarily, vague. 'Red-gold' will conjure a different colour to every reader and no two dragons would look quite the same if the book's many readers had the talent to draw what they thought they saw. This semantic fuzziness is absolutely crucial – at least as crucial as metonymy and synecdoche – in enabling language to work and it relies completely on the reader's individual creative powers: a thousand readers will create a thousand different dragons.

The final clause of the first half, 'fast asleep' helps us to grasp more fully the syntactic context of the word 'lay'. Lying asleep is meaningful. After the semi-colon things are further developed. 'A thrumming came from his jaws and nostrils' gives us a verb (thrumming) and a couple more nouns (jaws, nostrils). Thrumming, by metonymic association, gives breath to the dragon, and thus life. We all know what 'jaws' and 'nostrils' are, but, as with 'red-gold', precisely what we imagine, and hear, will depend on what we think a vast red-gold dragon looks like. The jaws and nostrils themselves are modified by their release of wisps of smoke, which, metonymically (reinforcing the 'thrumming') suggest the dragon's fire. This is rendered explicit in the final clause: 'but his fires were low in slumber'. This is, perhaps, the trickiest of the clauses to read by itself. Fire, of course, cannot sleep (just as, earlier, we noted it cannot die). So we have a metaphor: the *vehicle* is slumber, the *tenor* is fire, and the *ground* is a temporary suspension of activity. The important aspect of its semantic context is temporariness – that is, the fire could, metaphorically, awaken. It's worth noting the plural here – 'his fire*s*' – which intensifies this threat. But we also have this strange word 'low'. Again, this is a dead metaphor for a certain state of fire ('the fire had burned low'), but, rather unusually, in this context it seems literal – that is, the dragon's fires are 'sleeping' low down in his body, only the fumes escaping. The semantic context allows this ambiguity to exist and the full sense of the sentence rather relies on it. As readers we do all that creative picturing almost without thinking, as the grammar does its silent work across the time it takes to read the sentence. But as we come to understand the *syntactic context*, the ways words work with each other to generate meaning, we realise how complex even the simplest literary sentence is likely to be, and how the act of reading hides a multitude of complexities.

COMPLEXITY CASE STUDY

Some literary sentences we can hardly even hope to be simple; those, for example, written by Shakespeare. The following is a case in point: 'Good Hamlet, cast thy nighted colour off/And let thine eye look like a friend on Denmark.' (1.2.68–69) Just seventeen words, only one comma, and all familiar words, even if the second person singular possessive pronouns 'thy' and 'thine' are hardly current. Even so, it is almost futile to try to understand what most of these words mean outside of a larger context. The name 'Hamlet' has – rather like 'dragon' – a broad cultural relevance well beyond the play that bears his name. But in what way is he 'good'? Here we need the historical dictionary to remind us that in the sixteenth and seventeenth centuries 'good' before a name would just be a polite form of address. As such it's rather empty, like the 'good' in Bilbo's 'good morning'. (The *OED* gives more than forty definitions for the word 'good', many of which have over a dozen subsections; some of those subsections have subsections.) 'Cast' is another word with several possible meanings if left to its own devices: the players of a play, something worn on a broken arm, a way of shaping metal, or of getting a baited hook into water. In order to make sense of it here we have to wait for the word 'off'. To 'cast off' has a nautical meaning, to set a boat free of its moorings, and it's a knitting term too. The *OED*, though, tells us that 'to throw off' is the most likely meaning as the sailing term doesn't become common until the late seventeenth century, and the knitting term the late nineteenth century. What, then, should be thrown away? Hamlet's 'nighted colour'. To turn the word 'night' into a verb is rather odd. Together 'nighted colour' suggests a colour that has been given the active qualities of night – it's a kind of metaphor. That is, Hamlet (the tenor) should throw away his 'nighted colour' (vehicle): but what is the ground? What about Hamlet has the qualities of night's colour? His clothes, his mood? Both are equally possible and there is a necessary ambiguity. Whichever it is, Hamlet is being asked to change something in his comportment, be it behaviour or dress; though the likelihood is both are connected.

There is a genuine grammatical ambiguity in the second line: 'And let thine eye look like a friend on Denmark'. This could mean that his 'eye' should resemble ('look like') a friend, that is a simile; or, and more likely, though much more complicatedly, that his eye is a synecdoche for a whole self and that Hamlet should act toward Denmark as a friend would. So what we have is ultimately a simile and a synecdoche pulling in the same direction. And, finally, what is 'Denmark', upon which Hamlet should look as a friend? Obviously a country; but also metonymically, it is the *king* of Denmark – though this couldn't be derived from the sentence itself. Indeed, and I'll explore this more fully in the next chapter, we need at least the essence of the whole scene – and perhaps the whole play – to make proper sense of even the smallest of its parts. What we have here, though, is a fine example of the way that just seventeen words can contain semantic and syntactic ambiguities, nouns turned into verbs, at least one metaphor and one simile, as well as both synecdoche and metonymy. It's quite wonderful what unpacking such a sentence reveals.

2 THE PARAGRAPH

In terms of working out how words hang together to create meaning in prose, the next thing up from the sentence is the paragraph. A paragraph is usually made up of one or more sentences which try to impart one idea or make one point. Take the following paragraph from fairly early on in a well-known novel we have already looked at:

> There was music from my neighbour's house through the summer nights. In his blue gardens men and girls came and went like moths among the whisperings and the champagne and the stars. At high tide in the afternoon I watched his guests diving from the tower of his raft, or taking the sun on the hot sand of his beach while his two motor-boats slit the waters of the Sound, drawing aquaplanes over cataracts of foam. On the week-ends his Rolls Royce became an omnibus, bearing parties to and from the city between nine in the morning and long past midnight, while his station wagon scampered like a brisk yellow bug to meet all trains. And on Mondays eight servants, including an extra gardener, toiled all day with mops and scrubbing-brushes and hammers and garden-shears, repairing the ravages of the night before.
>
> (39)

There are five sentences here, each building on the one before, to fill out the picture that we, as readers, are required to interpret. The first sentence is 'There was music from my neighbour's house through the summer nights.' So how does the information delivered by this sentence, which is made up of words that are easy to understand, but difficult to give any context to, develop? As it is, words like 'music' and 'neighbour's house', for example, could refer to any number of types of music or types of house. Equally, 'summer nights', while potentially evocative, has a very open semantic context: summer where? summer when? What is required is a wider syntactic context. The question is whether there's adequate syntactic context given in the rest of the paragraph alone to allow for a richer understanding.

The next sentence is completely different in tone and style: 'In his blue garden men and girls came and went like moths among the whisperings and the champagne and the stars.' Now, is this neighbour's garden literally 'blue'? Well, it could be in the sense that it's night-time and it's the blue of an expanse of grass lit by moonlight. But the word's semantic context is evocative of a mood: the blue notes of jazz music, perhaps; also a certain sadness. Through this night-coloured mood (compare Hamlet's 'nighted colour') move 'men and girls'. What's interesting here is that it's not men and *women*. The youth of the females is emphasised and implicitly contrasted with unspecified age of the men; this implies a certain power relationship that, when we think about the **adversarial context** later on, could be explored. Both men and girls come and go 'like moths', so the simile gives us a *tenor* of men and girls, a *vehicle* of moths, and a *ground* of things swiftly flickering, only half seen, drawn to the light through the dark. Then we realise that there are a lot of 'ands' (four in the sentence). The moth-like men and girls flutter through 'the whisperings and the champagne and the stars'. What we have here is a beaded string of metonymies. The whisperings evoke people; the champagne wealth and the stars the night. Together these metonymies, connected by that string of 'ands', begin to suggest glamour.

The next two sentences confirm this: first: 'At high tide in the afternoon I watched his guests diving from the tower of his raft, or taking the sun on the hot sand of his beach while his two motor-boats slit the waters of the Sound, drawing aquaplanes over cataracts of foam.' There is a slick non sequitur here – we've suddenly been moved from night to a sunny afternoon (or a series of them); and the metonymies of wealth and glamour continue: a raft with a tower, a beach and *two* motor-boats drawing aquaplanes (which are rather like wide single water skis). What is key here, though, is not the items themselves, but that as they are all *his* items they become metonymic of the elusive neighbour, the owner of the garden and all it contains. There are seven uses of 'his' in the paragraph and four of them in this sentence. In the next sentence this sense of wealth and glamour is further attached to the unnamed man: 'On the week-ends his Rolls Royce became an omnibus, bearing parties to and from the city between nine in the morning and long past midnight, while his station wagon scampered like a brisk yellow bug to meet all trains.' We are now being told about something that happens regularly – every weekend and the metonymy of wealth, indeed of what's becoming casual wealth – *his* Rolls Royce used as a bus morning and night. We are now being told about something that happens regularly – every weekend. This is reinforced by the unnamed person's casual use of wealth: *his* Rolls Royce, typically a metonymy for glamour, deployed as a mere bus morning and night.

Finally, in the last sentence of the paragraph, we return to the garden: 'And on Mondays eight servants, including an extra gardener, toiled all day with mops and scrubbing-brushes and hammers and garden-shears, repairing the ravages of the night before.' So the party is *temporarily* over – this happens every Monday – and a team of servants labour to repair the damage done by the rich and glamourous. The narrator thinks it important to tell us the number of servants, eight, and that there is 'an *extra* gardener'. In this way the chaos and destruction of the glamour class is, again metonymically, figured by the requirement to tidy it up, just so it can be disordered again (the parallel use of 'and' is suggestive of the connection between excess and destruction). Now, if we come back to the first sentence, we can only read it as a dramatic understatement: 'There was music from my neighbour's house through the summer nights.' The larger syntactic context changes our understanding of this initial sentence – enriches it and ironizes it. But the real achievement of our slow reading, drawing on the semantic and syntactic contexts, is to understand clearly and in detail just how literary prose can create a complex and layered world. There are, though, still things that cannot be understood in isolation. For example, who is the narrator? Who is the neighbour whose luxurious possessions are so suggestive? In this case the narrator is Nick Carraway and the neighbour a man by the name of Jay Gatsby. I'll come back to *The Great Gatsby* in later parts of this book.

3 FROM SYNTACTIC TO THEMATIC CONTEXTS

Having looked at some sentences that, though more or less complex, at least accord to the laws of grammar, it's worth recalling that writers are quite often rule breakers and disregard any such laws. We'll often see this in the English Renaissance, when the rules were still being shaped and were thus flexible; we'll also see it in a literary period of the late nineteenth and early twentieth century called Modernism, when rule breaking in some form was so commonplace it almost became a generic convention. Modernist writers were interested in challenging complacent reading habits. As such they can be useful for reminding us just what those habits are. We can explore this by looking at a poem by the American poet whose very name cannot be written without breaking a few rules – e. e. cummings:

since feeling is first
who pays any attention
to the syntax of things
will never wholly kiss you;

wholly to be a fool   5
while Spring is in the world

my blood approves,
and kisses are a better fate
than wisdom
lady i swear by all flowers. Don't cry   10
—the best gesture of my brain is less than
your eyelids' flutter which says

we are for each other: then
laugh, leaning back in my arms
for life's not a paragraph   15

And death i think is no parenthesis

(*Complete Poems* 292)

Reading something like this for the first time is a very strange experience. I would defy anyone to make full sense of such a poem on the basis of one reading – or even to enjoy it (except to the extent that befuddlement is an end in itself; like being drunk). When it comes to complexity on this scale, pleasure – which is more often than not linked in some way to mastery – can only emerge gradually as you work towards an understanding of it.

As you read it, and re-read it (not giving up on complexity is the first rule), and re-read it, what you'll probably notice is that many of the things you'd expect to be in a poem are missing: helpful punctuation, grammar, **rhythm, rhyme** – even sense. But, that said, there's not a single word in this poem that is either unusual or difficult. So what must be missing are the *contexts* for each of those words that, typically, allow meaning to happen;

namely the conventional ordering principles of the English language which we call syntax. If this is the case, then the semantic context of each word will have been liberated beyond our ability to contain it. Hence, we struggle to understand cummings' poem. Even so, 'since feeling is first' is clearly a poem. This is signified by the way the lines break off into space: perhaps the one sure sign that we are looking at a poem rather than prose, where line endings are decided by the typesetter. What we can say, then, is that we have a series of familiar words organised into some kind of poetic form.

How, then, can we make this poem work? I think one useful approach is to read it *slowly*, attending to the syntactic context, and see when and how (and maybe *if*) sense happens. As we don't have enough of the conventional markers of grammar to help us (capital letters, commas, full stops) we need to use what we do have as a structure, and that is the poetic line. Breaking it down line by line is a useful approach enabling us, as readers, to see meaning emerge.

The first line reads: 'since feeling is first'. There's no capital letter for 'since' suggesting that it's not, perhaps, a beginning. Something, presumably this 'feeling', is prior. But, though we might pause in reading briefly at the end of the line there is no punctuation point to force us to stop there and the word 'since' implies something to come, a change of state (since sentences often take the form: 'since x then y'). And we carry on: 'since feeling is first/who pays any attention'. A good reader is likely to be rather frustrated by something missing between these lines. If feels as though there should be either an extra word (like 'anyone') or a comma. As it is, though, we don't have that and have to think about what we *do* have. Certainly the 'who' has turned the momentum of the poem towards a question, but, again, the line doesn't complete its grammatical thrust enough for us not to ask 'attention to what?' A sentence that ran, with punctuation added, 'Since feeling is first, who pays any attention?' still doesn't quite work. The next line adds a bit more: 'since feeling is first/who pays any attention/to the syntax of things'. Now, suddenly, we have something that reads like a sentence, and as such a syntactic context for this initially confusing set of words. It is a question that can be re-written thus: 'Since feeling is first, who pays any attention to the syntax of things?' This certainly has the grammatical *form* of a question; but it's a very strange question.

What is 'the syntax of things'? 'Syntax', as I mentioned a few pages ago, comes from the Greek and means 'putting together in order'. So, we may understand the question as follows: because feeling is first (and thus more important) why should we give our attention to understanding the way things are ordered – just *feel*: that's enough. As a poetic sentiment that makes sense in and of itself: feeling is more important than understanding. The line, of course, in ignoring syntactical markers is mimicking this possible meaning.

However, there isn't a question mark here, and the poem carries on: 'since feeling is first/who pays any attention/to the syntax of things/will never wholly kiss you;'. After all our work stumbling through the first few lines, work demanded by the lack of grammatical markers, this last line changes everything. All of a sudden we have a love poem. As such unlocking the full syntactic context of those first lines gives us the poem's first *theme*: the sentiment that feeling outweighs understanding. That is consistent whether the poem is about love or not. It's just that now we know the feeling is passion. The speaker is telling his lover that they shouldn't think; they should just get on with things and enjoy them. This is the poem's **thematic context** and one we can pursue to begin to order the poem.

> We might add that the poem belongs to a tradition of *carpe diem* poetry – that is, 'seize the day'. This is its **generic context**. The most famous example is probably Andrew Marvell's 'To His Coy Mistress', but there is also 'From Far, From Eve and Morning' by A. E. Housman and 'Go, Lovely Rose' by Edmund Waller. In the cummings poem, though, there is, a pretty obvious irony: the reader needs to think *very* carefully about the syntax of the poem, the way the words are put together and ordered, in order to reconstruct this message.

With this **thematic context** in mind the rest of the poem becomes much more available. The next two lines, which form a separate stanza, run: 'wholly to be a fool/while Spring is in the world'. Again, this is hardly clear, but the theme helps us make sense of the lines. The speaker wants to be completely ('wholly') foolish (perhaps with the sense of 'fooling around' – i.e. sex – interestingly the *OED* dates the first usage of 'to fool' in this sense to 1923, three years before the publication of the poem); but not always, only during a given time period: 'while Spring is in the world'. Spring, here, carries the first capital letter in the poem, suggesting its importance. Spring typically figures creation, a sexual cycle, new life, the end of a cold period. If the vehicle is 'spring' and the tenor is the speaker's feeling, these are the sexual grounds of a metaphor. Another potential ground of spring, though, is that it's temporary. As such there is the now expected 'seize the day' element to the poem too, which limits the ground of the metaphor to mean sex *now*. But, again, there is no punctuation point at the end of this two-line stanza, and we need to take the meaning forward. The beginning of the next stanza tells us that it is the speaker's 'blood' that 'approves' this feeling. It is a physical rather than a mental passion. So the poem's two themes are emerging (and merging): the physical is more important that the intellectual; lovers need to grasp the moment.

The first theme is borne out by the next part of the poem, where 'kisses are a better fate/than wisdom'; and where the speaker's best thoughts ('the best gesture of [his] brain') is less than the physical 'flutter' of the lover's eyelids. There is a change of mood to be noted here, as the lover's eyelids seem to be fluttering away tears. Quite why the speaker has to ask the lover not to cry adds a dramatic tension to the poem. Now it could be that the lover is overwhelmed with desire and agrees with the speaker that they 'are for each other'; it could, however, be that the (potential?) lover is distressed. Though this will remain ambiguous, as we don't have enough context to make a firm decision, it does give us *the lover's* physical response and reminds us that there are two quite different people represented in the poem, one of whom may be resistant (as we shall see later, the **adversarial context** could cast a very different light on the speaker). This is also the point that more or less normal punctuation comes in (capital letter, dash, apostrophes, colon). It is, perhaps, as though the speaker needs to be clear to the lover, persuasive even, though again it's hard to be definitive.

In spite of the feelings of the other, the speaker wants to act intuitively and unreflectingly, and what we have throughout the poem is not just a conflict between feeling and thinking, but between feeling and the *representation* of feeling through writing – such as the structure of 'syntax'. It is as though writing – even a poem – will always fall short of expressing feeling, as writing is not life itself ('life's not a paragraph'). Here the poem becomes an extended metaphor for its own failure to capture passionate life. The *vehicle* is the poem, the *tenor* is feeling, and the *ground* is actually a kind of dissonance where feeling and poetry *don't* agree. The ground, unusually, is what the tenor and vehicle don't have in common. And, in the last line the speaker tells us that poetry also cannot capture death (presumably the end of feeling); though it does provide an interesting image: 'And death i think is no parenthesis.' Now, a parenthesis is a bracket, and what happens after a bracket (grammatically) is that the sentence picks up just where it left off. The speaker's last thought is that death, then, is not a picking up of the sentence. This is another negative metaphor: the *vehicle* is the parenthesis, the *tenor* is death, and the *ground* is what they *don't* have in common: one continues after a break, the other doesn't. This doesn't tell us what death *is*, but it certainly refuses to offer the reader much comfort. The lack of a full stop at the end of the poem, after 'parenthesis', implies something considerably more open than a return of the sentence. It also reflects back onto the *carpe diem* theme: we don't know what's next, so we better do what we do know now.

What a methodical slow reading allows is the gradual emergence of a variety of contexts which lets these everyday words become distinctively meaningful. As we move forward line by line we are able to use the thematic (and generic) contexts to construct a syntactic context that could give those early elusive lines meaning. From this emerged two themes: feeling v. thought and *carpe diem*. As we progressed, placing later lines which made little sense in and of themselves into these contexts uncovered a drama of sexual persuasion, and possibly passionate love, which runs: life is short, we don't know what's next; we need to grab our moment, ignore our tears, and love without thought. Re-reading the poem now is a very different – indeed a *pleasurable* – experience. But perhaps more pleasure has been generated by the process of analysis itself.

CAN YOU OVER-READ?

Before moving on to the next section, something that needs be thought about is just how much detail any critical analysis can afford to go into. Seventeen words of Shakespeare initiated five hundred words of interpretation. Sixteen lines of e. e. cummings yielded over fifteen hundred words. In neither of these cases would I claim to be anything like complete in my analysis. It's very probable that the complete analysis of any piece of literary language is impossible. It's not even particularly desirable. What's really important is that the piece of language under investigation becomes richer and more vital and that our ability to grasp its pleasures emerges with increased clarity and presence. What any method of literary analysis needs is a judgment between offering detailed readings of small parts of a work alongside evidence that those details are understood to be part of a larger context – that of the work as a whole. I avoided this with the sentence from *Hamlet*, but began to show how it could be done with the analysis of 'since feeling is first'. Here I spent a lot of time on the beginning, setting out how each part can be better understood with reference to the poem's thematic context, then moved a little more quickly through the middle of the poem, and then gave a more detailed interpretation of the last line. Beginnings and ends are always worth giving time to; but what really matters is being able to give that sense of the *whole*. So, I would say, over-reading is unlikely to be a problem. The more typical issue is *under*-reading which fails to account for the relationship between the parts of a text and its whole. Almost always it is the thematic context that enables such a reading to work.

SUMMARY AND THE RE-READING CYCLE

I've said a few times now that the only reading that can generate an effective close reading is *re*-reading. This is because what we are looking for in close reading are patterns: the ways words relate to each other, their semantic and syntactic contexts, and the way those relationships work out across a text to develop a thematic context. As you re-read, these patterns become clearer and clearer and mutually reinforce each other because you achieve increased control over at least some of any given text's possible meanings. At the end of a first read you may experience a mixture of things, amongst which are likely to be: strong images and 'sounds', memories of characters and particular events, a loose sense of the plot, a strong feeling that a lot of what you spent good time reading has evaporated, satisfaction and relief at having finished (if it was long or difficult), disappointment at having finished (if it was very good, or, for a different reason, if it was very bad), and so on. Ideally, most of these feelings will be pleasurable. Nevertheless, usually (depending on *how* you read) this mixture will be unanalysed – more or less a stew of bits and pieces. Re-reading should enhance each of those feelings: character and its relationship to the plot will become clearer; significant events will be more obvious as you can see where they are leading (the **thematic context**); the language of the work will become more available for consideration (the **semantic** and **syntactic context**); your feelings on completion should come into a sharper focus as you will be beginning to possess the work; you will retain more of the information yielded by the pages of the book. Each re-read will intensify this feeling of pleasure and power. A methodical reading and re-reading of a work will increase the speed at which you gain control of a given text and, moreover, enable you to explain more successfully what it is that you know.

As I've been putting the reading experience together so far in this guide, an ideal re-reading cycle, drawing on the methods outlined so far, should work as follows. You start off with the unread whole lying before you, then as you read you begin to attend to the words, then the sentences, then the lines, stanza and/or paragraphs; from this you work out, intuitively, the images, characters, the actions, the themes, which give you a broad, but unanalysed sense of a newly read whole. Then, as you *re-read* you can start to think about how that whole determines whether any of the semantic context of specific words may be interesting, what sentences, phrases, lines, etc., may come into focus and how these fit into slightly larger syntactic contexts like paragraphs, stanzas, chapters or scenes. From your sense of how these fit together you'll build up a more nuanced idea of the thematic context. This will then give you a richer sense of the whole. At which point you may go round the cycle again, enhancing your understanding of each context with your own increased knowledge. It might not surprise you to note that for those works that have become 'classic' works of fiction or poetry this cycle is almost certainly endlessly repeatable; but, moreover, this repetition leads to endless difference. There is no such thing, thankfully, as a definitive reading of a literary text.

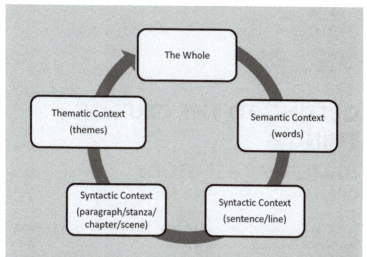

Figure 3.1

Such a re-reading process would look like the scheme in Figure 3.1. Here, as the reading the reading cycle is undertaken, the whole – that is, the meaning of a work that your best interpretation can deliver – constantly evolves as each part of the cycle is revisited and the richness and complexity of the reading experience is fully enjoyed.

FURTHER READING

Reuben Brower. 'Reading in Slow Motion', in *In Defense of Reading*. Eds Reuben Brower and Richard Poirier. New York: Dutton, 1962.

Tom Furniss and Michael Bath. *Reading Poetry: An Introduction*. 2nd edn. London: Longman, 2007.

Winifred Nowottny. *The Language Poets Use*. London: Athlone, 1962.

I. A. Richards. *How to Read a Page*. London: Routledge. 1957.

Shira Wolosky. *The Art of Poetry: How to Read a Poem*. Oxford: Oxford University Press, 2001.

4

GETTING TO THE CRUX OF THINGS

HAMLET, A CASE STUDY

So far the opening three chapters have introduced and demonstrated several way of reading short works, such as poems, and extracts of longer works, such as sentences and paragraphs, using three of the contexts of close reading, the **semantic**, the **syntactic** and the **thematic**. What I want to do now is show you how these work together in an extended case study: a close reading of Act 1, Scene 2 from Shakespeare's *Hamlet*. In order to do this I shall carefully work through the re-reading cycle outlined at the end of the last section. This begins with a sense of the whole – even if it's as rudimentary as a plot outline. Then I shall rehearse the various contexts and elaborate on their interrelationships with each other. With this inter-relationship in mind, I shall introduce you to one further idea that is useful in larger scale analyses. This is something that for the purposes of this guide I'm calling the **crux**. A crux, as I am using it here, is a point in a text where two or more of the contexts of close reading are at work together. They occur at points of particular literary density and very often make very effective foci for advanced close reading and, when understood, offer that frisson of pleasure.

1 A SENSE OF THE WHOLE: *HAMLET*'S PLOT

The main thrust of the plot of *Hamlet* can be summarised as follows. Hamlet's father (also called Hamlet) has been killed by his brother, Claudius. Claudius swiftly married the old king's wife (and young Hamlet's mother) Gertrude. Hamlet, already despondent at his father's death and mother's quick marriage, becomes vengeful when he learns from the ghost of his father that it was his uncle Claudius who had murdered him. In order to enact his revenge Hamlet pretends to be mad. Despite the success of this ruse (everybody does think he is mad) Hamlet is unable to kill Claudius because his conscience bothers him and he is unsure of Claudius' guilt. He explores his thoughts about his conscience, the corruption of men and women, and his own failings, in a number of soliloquies and in conversation with his old school friends Rosencrantz and Guildenstern and his close friend Horatio. The plan Hamlet comes up with to ascertain Claudius' guilt is a play within a play. He gets a troop of visiting players to imitate the murder of his father with Claudius in the audience. Claudius reacts like a guilty man and Hamlet is finally sure of what he should do. However, before he can act he is summoned to see his mother. There he inadvertently kills Polonius, the King's counsellor, who was hidden behind an arras, mistaking him for Claudius. He has a charged confrontation with his mother – accusing her directly of sexual corruption. He is now deemed not only mad but dangerous and sent to England with Rosencrantz and Guildenstern, who have instructions from the King for Hamlet's execution. There are two key sub-plots both involving Polonius' children, Ophelia and Laertes. The first is centred on Ophelia, who had been Hamlet's lover. Ophelia is told by her father towards the beginning of the play to reject Hamlet and she does; this adds to Hamlet's own emotional distraction, especially his consciousness of the corruptibility of women, and it becomes increasingly unclear whether he is mad or only pretending to be. When Ophelia learns that Hamlet has killed her father she goes mad and drowns herself in a river. The second subplot involves Laertes. When Laertes hears of his father's death he storms back to Elsinore and demands immediate justice. Claudius convinces Laertes that Hamlet was to blame not only for his father's death but also for Ophelia's death. When Hamlet returns to Denmark having sent his school friends to their deaths in his place, Claudius comes up with a plan for Laertes and Hamlet to have a fencing competition. A vengeful Laertes poisons his blade and strikes Hamlet, poisoning him. In the subsequent skirmish the blades get swapped and Hamlet unknowingly poisons Laertes. As a backup Claudius had poisoned a drink. The queen accidentally drinks this and dies, though not before accusing Claudius of adding the poison. Enraged at his mother's death

Hamlet runs Claudius through with the poisoned blade. Hamlet, Claudius, Laertes and Gertrude all die.

This, of course, is not a close reading; it's a broad summary the only purpose of which is to enable you as a reader to move reasonably confidently across the play as a whole. This is the kind of knowledge that a 'good reader' has in the back of their minds when they are looking at any particular parts of the play's language. It is what one might call a macro-context for each of its individual elements. Ascertaining which elements are ripe for more detailed analysis is a case of careful judgment. As I go through the close reading I shall try to explain and justify my choices against three criteria:

CRITERIA FOR CLOSE READING

1   That at least one, though preferably more than one, of the contexts of close reading can be used to open them up – where possible I shall focus on 'cruxes';

2   That each example is helpful in opening up the text more widely – that is, each example is part of a larger pattern (e.g. a thematic context);

3   That all the examples relate to each other and create a progressive reading of the scene in question, leading to the pleasure of mastery.

Now I have outlined the plot of *Hamlet*, I shall move incrementally through the gears of the various contexts of close reading, demonstrating how they can be used to give a reading that draws the disparate parts of Act 1, Scene 2 together.

2 THE CRUX: SEMANTIC AND THEMATIC CONTEXTS

At the outset of Act 1, Scene 2 the newly crowned King Claudius addresses the court with the following words: 'Though yet of Hamlet our dear brother's death/The memory be green' (*Hamlet* 1.2.1–2). The word 'green' here immediately appears strange, which draws our attention to it. Just what semantic context could give it a meaning and in what ways might that meaning be enhanced if we see 'green' as a **crux** when aligned with other contexts of close reading? Now, it is pretty clear that a memory cannot *literally* be green. 'Green' is meant figuratively and, to draw again on Richards' formula, memory is the *tenor*, green is the *vehicle* and we need to discover the *ground*. That is, which of green's many and various qualities and connotations are relevant. This is when we need to know something of the macro-context – in this case, the plot. One thing that matters is that King Hamlet, Claudius' brother, has only recently died. Thus, perhaps we might guess at 'freshness' and/or 'vitality' and/or 'rawness' as the ground suggesting that the memory is both recent and has a lively, even tender, presence (it's interesting that this piece of figurative language seems to lead only to other equally figurative substitutions – as though there is no common literal word for this kind of feeling). These different grounds work in different ways. 'Freshness' suggests a kind of tenderness, 'rawness' a kind of discomfort, 'vitality' would connote a living presence. All of them are able to point towards much stronger feelings than a literal word like 'present' would be able to do. So the metaphor works at that level, the level of complex *feeling*. We might also want to think about the setting of the delivery – its semantic situation. This is a court scene – and thus Claudius is making a political speech. He wants to evoke a certain feeling in his audience, to get them to feel with him and control their emotions. Claudius is, after all, an exemplary politician and keenly aware of some, if not all, of the possibilities of his metaphors.

That he is unaware of *all* of the connotations of green may well prove interesting. What, perhaps more hidden, grounds of 'green' are there? Well, sickness, corruption, jealousy to name but a few. (Because of the text's historical context we can exclude contemporary meanings like 'go' or 'environmentalism'.) Could these also be relevant? Do we have a case here of ambiguity? Well, to the plot again. We know that the speaker, Claudius, was also the killer of King Hamlet and that he rather quickly assumed his crown and married his wife. Could his memory then suggest jealousy? Yes. Could it suggest corruption and sickness – yes again, and all the more so as he poisoned his brother in a way that suggests his body would have been instantly corrupted (the ghost recalls how his blood was turned to 'curd' and his body covered with a 'vile and loathsome crust' [1.5.69, 73]). We will also know that 'Something is rotten in the state of Denmark' (1.4.90) and that corruption is a major thematic context of the play, coming up again and again in its imagery (this light touch use of supporting quotation can be very effective way of demonstrating a fuller grasp of the play). So after analysis we have a rather complex situation as a variety of contexts are all relevant and can be argued for. As an example of a crux, then, 'green' might mean one thing to the court to whom this speech is addressed, such as the sharing of a fresh grief, and quite another to the speaker, whose conscience is exposing itself through its metaphorical choices, and yet another to the playwright, whose mind is occupied with particular themes. It all depends on just how richly we grasp the contexts which can determine − and keep open − the ground.

COMPLEXITY CASE STUDY

We can though, with dense literary language, almost always take things further. How do we get from green to, say, freshness? Green is a colour, not a quality of life. That's to say green, when used to mean 'freshness' or 'vitality' is *already* being used figuratively. But in what way? Is it a metaphor? In which case what would be the tenor, vehicle and ground? I suppose freshness would be the *tenor*, green would remain the *vehicle* and life would be the *ground*. That said, is 'greenness' a quality of life in the same way that 'fierceness', for example, is a quality of a lion? No it isn't. So, I would argue (and others may disagree − that's really the point of good criticism: it always leaves open a space for reasonable contradiction), what we are dealing with isn't a metaphor, but a **metonym**. In the case of Claudius' speech greenness is *associated* with life but is not a *quality* of life. Life, then, has a metonymic relationship with the colour green through association, for example, with the new growth of plant life and general verdancy (a word which is rooted in Old French and Latin words for 'green'; *OED*). Indeed, on closer inspection our metaphorical analysis of green turns into a metonymic analysis and all of green's associations, such as sickness, jealousy, and corruption, even where these may be literally green (as with sickness and corruption) and excessive growth, what Hamlet calls 'an unweeded garden/That grows to seed' (1.2.134–135).

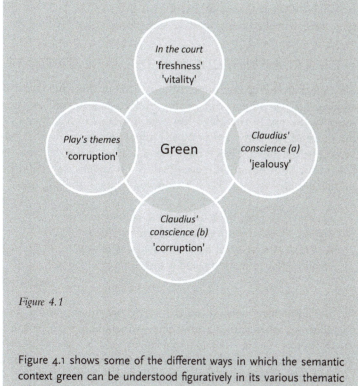

Figure 4.1

Figure 4.1 shows some of the different ways in which the semantic context green can be understood figuratively in its various thematic contexts.

So how has this worked? Beginning at the beginning, I chose to reflect on the odd word 'green', and its plausible meanings within its semantic context (the situations of the court, conscience, the play as a whole), and as a piece of unusual figurative language (metaphor/metonymy). For Claudius the memory of his brother could be vital, fresh, jealous *and* corrupted. The word 'green' is, then, clearly a **crux**; that is, a place in the language of the work where the semantic and the thematic contexts overlap yielding a particularly rich potential for meaning. Identifying cruxes, those places where more than one contexts is productive, is, as shown here, one key to effective close reading. Usually cruxes only stand out on repeat readings of a work, or at least, only when a reasonable understanding of a work has been reached. If you can spot them you should always have something to say.

3 THE CRUX: SYNTACTIC AND THEMATIC CONTEXTS

Though there's certainly more to be said about the King's courtly address, for the purposes of getting to Hamlet's words, and into some of the joy of the play's language, I want to concentrate on the entry of the play's hero. What's important plot wise is as follows: Hamlet doesn't yet know that Claudius has murdered his father, but he is profoundly disturbed by his father's death and his mother's swift marriage. He is introduced in the following lines:

> *Claudius*   But now, my cousin Hamlet, and my son –
> *Hamlet*   A little more than kin, and less than kind.
> *Claudius*   How is it that the clouds still hang on you?
> *Hamlet*   Not so much my, lord, I am too much in the 'son'.
>
> (1.2.64–67)

In the immediate context of the scene we might notice that Claudius has taken rather a long time – including a conversation about Laertes' future – to get to Hamlet, and he begins with a 'But' – as though even then it's an afterthought. Actors can do a lot with that kind of thing; critics have to wait and see if it becomes relevant. Another context to be born in mind is the semantic context for the word 'cousin', which may seem a bit unusual as Claudius is either Hamlet's uncle or his stepfather. But, according to the *OED*, in and around 1600 it meant: 'A collateral relative more distant than a brother or sister; a kinsman or kinswoman, a relative; formerly very frequently applied to a nephew or niece'. It became limited to its current meaning sometime in the eighteenth century. This historical element of the semantic context is important because Claudius' line moves from this more distant relationship to 'son'. There is something ingratiating in that movement which echoes the uncomfortable transformation from uncle to father.

Hamlet's first line reflects this discomfort: 'A little more than kin and less than kind'. The first part of his opening line, 'A little more than kin', is far from straightforward, but his use of 'kin' is clearly picking up on Claudius' reference to their family connection. He is saying something like: Claudius as *father* is too close a kinship relation for him to accept. The second part of the line, 'and less than kind', which first plays on the sound connection between 'kin' and 'kind', contains the 'less' necessary to balance out the 'more', and raises at least two of kind's meanings: to be of a similar type and to be pleasant. It seems to mean that though Claudius may *claim* close kinship with Hamlet, Hamlet sees Claudius and himself as *less* than similar, and Claudius' claim that they are, as *less* than pleasant. The syntactic context definitely encourages this ambiguity in 'kind'. Hamlet is not being unclear, he is being clever. This sort of wordplay in itself would not mean that much, but if we see it become a consistent pattern then it becomes part of Hamlet's 'character' and thus significant on that account (we'll look at this kind of thing in more detail when we come to the **iterative context** in the next two chapters).

Claudius' response is a question which doesn't seem to take any account of what Hamlet has said: 'How is it that the clouds still hang on you?' This *non sequitur* could be deliberate – e.g., I'll say what I was going to say anyway, or I'll ignore your rudeness as this is a public forum; or it could be ignorance, i.e., I'm not really listening to anyone but myself right now. Again, any of these interpretations are possible – but which is most likely will depend on what we learn of Claudius. My own view would be it's a mixture of the first two. We should have learned from his earlier speeches that Claudius is too shrewd politically not to listen and too careful about his public presentation to bandy words with Hamlet. Rather he asks, in front of the court, a direct question. Claudius doesn't use wordplay, but, as before, the semantic context of his language is figurative: the 'clouds' cannot literally be hanging on Hamlet. If we apply Richards' formulation, the *tenor* is Hamlet's demeanour, the *vehicle* is the clouds, and the *ground* is a dreary darkness. The cause of this isn't yet settled by the play, but we do know his father has recently died, so we can begin to speculate and refine our position as we gain more knowledge through the re-reading cycle.

Hamlet's response directly alludes to his lost father and again picks up on Claudius' own figure: 'Not so much, my lord, I am too much in the son.' Here – and perhaps we are beginning to see a pattern – Hamlet uses clever wordplay both to extend Claudius' meteorological metaphor and to satirise his claim to be his father. That said, the meaning is rather obscure. The extension of Claudius' cloud metaphor suggests that we should hear 'sun' rather than 'son' (of course, as both words *sound* the same this would be indistinguishable to the court audience and to the theatre audience), but in our text we have 'son'. The fact that we have 'son' means that we, as close readers, have to work out its semantic context through the syntactic context. I would suggest it means something like 'the claim that I am your son is too much'. However, the *Folio* version of the play, published eighteen years after the second *Quarto* version I'm using here, and seven years after Shakespeare's death, gives us 'I am too much i'th'Sun.' There is, unfortunately, no way of telling which text has the greater authority, but the case for 'sun' could certainly be made on the strength of the imagery. However we read the line it tells us that Hamlet cannot resist wordplay, even if it doesn't always quite work. We have two cases of it in his first two lines.

This compulsive wordplay happens again a few lines later when Hamlet picks up on his mother's use of the word 'common' to mean 'everyday' at line 72, 'Thou knowst 'tis common all that lives must die' and, if we maintain the tone from Hamlet's conversation with Claudius, transforms the word to mean something more like 'vulgar' at line 74: 'Ay, madam, it is common'. As such we can see that character is emerging through **iteration**. And it occurs again in the passage of dialogue, which follows directly:

Queen:	If it be. Why seems it so particular with thee?	75
Hamlet:	'Seems', madam – nay it is, I know not 'seems'.	
	'Tis not alone my inky cloak, cold mother,	
	Nor customary suits of solemn black,	
	Nor windy suspiration of forced breath,	
	Nor the fruitful river in the eye,	80
	Nor the dejected haviour of the visage,	
	Together with all forms, moods, shapes of grief,	
	That can denote me truly. These indeed might 'seem',	
	For they are actions that a man might play,	

> But I have that within which passes show,   85
> These but the trappings and the suits of woe.
>
> (1.2.74–86)

The ordinary English word 'seem' is repeated four times in these dozen or so lines; three times in the first three lines then again at line 83. This would suggest that its semantic context is worthy of consideration. The syntactic context of the first usage is 'If it be/ Why *seems* it so with particular with thee?' To begin with we need to recall what the queen's 'it' refers to. The context makes it pretty clear that it's the 'commonness' of death. It must be very uncomfortable to hear your own mother tell you that your father's death shouldn't matter (be 'so particular') to you, a son, just because death is 'common'. When the queen asks why Hamlet is taking his father's death so badly she uses 'seem' in the sense of 'having the appearance of', an expression which always contains the possibility that something *appears* different from what it *is*; as though she can't quite believe that he does care this much. And it's this that Hamlet picks up on: '"Seems", madam – nay it is, I know not "seems."' Hamlet is making a distinction between the verbs 'to seem' and 'to be'; and in so doing he is giving us a potential thematic context (*seeming* v. *being*). The re-reading cycle will confirm this. While there's no hard evidence that the queen was doubting Hamlet's honest expression of grief, his sensitivity to her words' semantic contexts infers that doubt – hence the 'cold mother' at line 77.

In order to work through this thematic distinction between *being* and *seeming*, Hamlet provides a long list of things that give the outward *appearance* of feeling: dark clothes, sighs, tears, anguished looks (he uses the word 'nor' to begin four consecutive lines). All these, he notes, 'are actions that a man might play'. These 'might "seem"'. They can be performed, that is, acted. But there is, Hamlet claims, no *essential* connection between inner life and outer behaviour; between 'forms' and that which could 'denote [him] truly'. In terms of what we have been discussing, what Hamlet has discovered is a problem with **metonymy** – that is, with taking an association for the thing it's associated with. Mourning clothes can be worn by those who do not feel grief, but only wish to show it. Tears and sighs may mean sadness, but can also be acted. Such outward signs of grief as performed for the court are, in effect, metonymic. The court is a place of show, of ceremony, or decorum and right behaviour. It is not a place for self-revelation. Hamlet's lines, refuting this metonymic conduct, are not only in keeping with his earlier quipping with the king about kin and kind, but are also a challenge to such courtly actions as shown, for example, by Claudius' 'Though yet of Hamlet our dear brother's death/The memory be green'. This suggests that it is the mere performance of grief and as such that it is a transitory 'mood' rather than a deeper change of being.

Hamlet's refusal to deliver the right kind of public behaviour demonstrates how out of place Hamlet is in this courtly environment; and, begins to suggest how out of place, indeed, how unwanted, honesty is in that setting. His final claim is that he 'has that within which passes show,/These but the trappings and the suits of woe'. This creates an interesting problem: how can a playwright or an actor 'show' that which 'passes show'? *All* an actor has is *show*: performed behaviour and actions of various kinds. These 'actions' are the very things that an audience (at a court or theatre) would understand as grief through their presentation alone. All, then, that an actor can do is exploit the very 'forms, moods and shapes of grief' that Hamlet rejects as capable of self-projection. This seems to energise a new thematic context: what is it to represent the self on stage (be it the court in the play or the theatre the play is in) when performance is, by its very nature, metonymic – based on the imitation of recognisable traits. What, then, is it *to be*, rather than *to seem*? An answer to this problem is found in the soliloquy. This connects the thematic context of being and seeming to the thematic context of acting, further enriching our interpretation of the play's words.

4 THE CRUX: SEMANTIC, SYNTACTIC AND THEMATIC CONTEXTS

I want to finish this section by considering a soliloquy in some detail. When we are dealing with a Shakespearean soliloquy we are analysing language at its very highest intensity – where cruxes will be common. Being selective in any analysis is particularly important. One approach to this is to focus on already identified thematic, semantic and syntactic contexts (though being aware that a soliloquy is likely to raise new ideas too). These should be based on what you have already discovered. So, in this case, we have the thematic contexts of (a) corruption, and (b) being/ seeming and acting. Each of these will have very specific effects on the semantic and syntactic contexts; that is, the way we interpret certain words' meanings, such as figurative language. Focusing on these few things as we are coming to understand them makes the soliloquy more manageable.

Here it is in its entirety:

O that this too too sallied flesh would melt,
Thaw and resolve itself into a dew,   130
Or that the Everlasting had not fixt
His canon 'gainst self-slaughter. O God, God,
How weary, stale, flat, and unprofitable
Seem to me all the uses of this world!
Fie on't, ah, fie, 'tis an unweeded garden   135
That grows to seed, things rank and gross in nature
Possess it merely. That it should come thus:
But two months dead – nay not so much, not two –
So excellent a king, that was to this
Hyperion to a satyr, so loving to my mother,   140
That he might not beteem the winds of heaven
Visit her face too roughly. Heaven and earth,
Must I remember? Why, she should hang on him
As if increase of appetite had grown
By what it fed on, and yet within a month,   145
(Let me not think on't – Frailty thy name is Woman),
A little month, or e'er those shoes were old
With which she followed my poor father's body,
Like Niobe all tears. Why, she –
O God, a beast that wants discourse of reason   150
Would have mourned longer, married with my uncle,
My father's brother (but no more like my father
Than I to Hercules). Within a month,
Ere yet the salt of most unrighteous tears,
Had left the flushing in her galled eyes   155
She married. O most wicked speed! To post

With such dexterity to incestuous sheets,
It is not, nor it cannot come to good;
But break, my heart, for I must hold my tongue.

(1.2.129–159)

Bearing in mind the themes and other contexts of close reading we're looking for (corruption, being/seeming, acting, figurative language), I've requoted the soliloquy below in a 'marked up' form where the thematic context of corruption is in *italics* and being and seeming/acting is in **bold**; the semantic context's figurative language is underlined. I've also broken the soliloquy into its sentences to help identify the syntactic context. This should also simplify the identification of cruxes.

O that this too too *sallied flesh would melt,*
Thaw and resolve itself into a dew,   130
Or that the Everlasting had not fixt
His canon 'gainst self-slaughter.
                                    O God, God,
How *weary, stale, flat, and unprofitable*
Seem to me all the uses of this world!

Fie on't, ah, fie, 'tis an unweeded garden   135
That grows to seed, things rank and gross in nature
Possess it merely.
                            That it should come thus:
But two months dead – nay not so much, not two –
So excellent a king, that was to this
Hyperion to a satyr, so loving to my mother,   140
That he might not beteem the winds of heaven
Visit her face too roughly.
                            Heaven and earth,
Must I remember?
                        Why, she should hang on him
As if increase of appetite had grown
By what it fed on, and yet within a month,   145
(Let me not think on't – *Frailty* thy name is Woman),
A little month, or e'er those shoes were old
With which she followed my poor father's body,

> **Like Niobe all tears**.
>> Why, she –
> O God, a *beast that wants discourse of reason*   150
> *Would have mourned longer,* married with my uncle,
> My father's brother (but no more like my father
> Then I to Hercules).
>> Within a month,
> Ere yet the **salt of most unrighteous tears,**
> **Had left the flushing in her galled eyes**   155
> She married.
>> O most *wicked* speed!
>>> To post
> With such dexterity to *incestuous sheets*,
> It is not, nor it cannot come to good;
> But break, my heart, for I must hold my tongue.
>
>>>> (1.2.129–159)

What I would want to draw attention to here are those areas where there is more than one thing going on, which I've called cruxes. A **crux,** as defined above, is where context affects meaning in more than one way – e.g., thematically *and* semantically. In this extract I have identified five such cruxes, at lines 129–130, 135–137, and 157 on the theme of corruption and 148 and 154–156 on the theme of being/seeming, each also containing metaphor, metonym or another figurative form. We can now work through these in order, beginning with corruption and then thinking about being and seeming. It would be ideal if analysis could also discover a connection between them. When undertaking a close reading it's nearly always a good idea to go through the piece in order. I can find no reason to make an exception here.

(A) CRUXES OF CORRUPTION

It's a bit of a shame that the first lines of the soliloquy, which contain the first crux, also present the greatest challenge: 'O that this too too sallied flesh would melt,/Thaw and resolve itself into a dew'. The basic image provided by the language is fairly straightforward: that flesh would change its state into something purer. The complexity, though, lies with the word 'sallied'. According to the *OED* 'sallied' means assailed or besieged. As this is unlikely to be literal, we are dealing with a figurative expression, here a metaphor. This is slightly complicated by the additional use of a synecdoche of 'flesh', which is used to represent all of Hamlet. With respect to sallied: the *tenor* is Hamlet (allowing for the synecdoche), the *vehicle* is 'sallied flesh' and the *ground* is Hamlet's feeling of being besieged and under attack in the court. This semantic context is complex but quite understandable. However, we have already seen with 'son/sun' there is more than one version of *Hamlet*. In the later *Folio* version the word 'sallied' becomes 'solid'. In many ways this more successfully fits the imagery as something that is solid can 'melt' and 'thaw' (as the *Folio*'s 'sun' was arguably preferable to the second *Quarto*'s 'son' earlier in the scene). It saves us from the mixed metaphor of something besieged then melting. However, the proliferation of meaning doesn't stop there. Other editors of the text have, drawing on what we might now call thematic and syntactic contexts, opted for 'sullied' – assuming that the typesetters may have mistaken an *u* for an *a*. Again, this beautifully fits the thematic context of corruption (much more clearly than 'sallied') and makes sense of the syntactic context of purification, the resolution 'into a dew'. One of the real pleasures of *reading* Hamlet is that, as a reader, you can have *all* of these meanings at work at once, each enriching the character of Hamlet and adding to, rather than diminishing, the play's potential for meaning. Does Hamlet feel besieged, that is at war with the court? Does he feel too 'fleshy', with the overtones of a Christian rejection of the carnal body? Does he feel dirty, having taken on the rottenness of Denmark? As a reader you can see the three words and their different meanings hovering over each other, vying for your attention, creating a kind of interpretative frisson, deepening your engagement with the language of the play. Context determines meaning, but it doesn't necessarily limit it. Such are the pleasures of ambiguity.

The next crux relating to the theme of corruption is at lines 135– 137, Hamlet's reflection on the state of the 'this world': ''tis an unweeded garden/That grows to seed, things rank and gross in nature/Possess it merely'. This is an extended metaphor in which the tenor is the 'world', the vehicle 'an unweeded garden', and the ground the connotations of a lack of order and care. These connotations are modified by the semantic context of the word 'rank', which, according to the *OED* around 1600 meant rotten, and, paradoxically, vigorous growth. Together they suggest energetic and even luxuriant corruption. At that time 'rank' also connoted moral evil, which gives this very material scene a spiritual dimension. The way that these meanings differ and yet combine is fascinating, demonstrating once more how poetry opens up semantic contexts to their potential. The other modifier is 'gross', which, again according to the *OED*, meant excessive growth as well as unwholesomeness. In many ways in this context rank and gross mean the same thing. This is an example of a 'hendiadys', an unusual rhetorical form, but one very prominent in *Hamlet*, where two similar words are used in the same figure ('trappings/suits' is another example at 1.2.86). It has an intensifying effect, but also creates a kind of reverberation between meanings which increases productive ambiguity.

(B) CRUXES OF CORRUPTION, BEING, SEEMING *AND* ACTING

A valid question here is what Hamlet means by 'world' as it gives us a contextual range for the meanings of the other words. Does he mean the earth in its entirety, or the world of the court – that is, of Elsinore under his uncle's rule? It's quite plausible that he means both – the court is the corrupt world in miniature. It's also worth reflecting on Hamlet's use of 'seem' at line 134. It's not a crux as such, but as it connects this passage to the forgoing conversation with his mother it could be important: 'How weary, stale, flat, and unprofitable/Seem to me all the uses of this world!' Is there a difference here between being and seeming, connected to the thematic context outlined above? If we say yes to this then Hamlet's views are merely subjective – how things *appear* to him. If we say no then Hamlet is just responding to a fallen world. One of the things that's most attractive to readers of *Hamlet* is actually the likelihood of the former: Hamlet's perspective on the world *creates* the sense of darkness and corruption rather than responds to it (we saw this with Romeo and Juliet in the first chapter). Also (and especially if we recall the reading of the opening line to include 'sullied') Hamlet is not distancing himself from this corruption, as though he is above it or outside it. His flesh is one with the matter of the 'unweeded garden'.

Just what it is that Hamlet is responding to becomes clear in the final 'corruption' crux: the 'incestuous sheets'. Here the semantic context of 'sheets' metonymically signify the marriage bed of this mother and uncle, and using a second order metonym, bed figures sex; and 'incestuous' refers to the situation where a sister-in-law and a brother-in-law have sexual relations with each other. Such a relationship was forbidden under Christian law, so, though technically incorrect as they are not biologically brother and sister, Hamlet's accusation does have some validity. The charge of corruption, the thematic context, is in this case aimed specifically at his mother. Hamlet's use of the word 'dexterity' ('To post/With such dexterity to incestuous sheets') is worth opening up with respect to Gertrude. On the one hand, the *OED* tells us that around 1600 'dexterity' meant cleverness, with the connotations of taking advantage of a situation; on the other hand it meant a kind of bodily skill. The first suggests that it's Gertrude who takes advantage of her husband's death to become entangled with Claudius; the second that her bedroom activities are particularly skilful. Either of these alone could appal a son; both together could be more than doubly damaging, creating Hamlet's view of the 'unprofitable' world. Moreover this is only the final slur against his 'cold mother' in this soliloquy; two of the others are cruxes where figurative language is tied to the theme of acting. This in turn yields a broader crux: Gertrude as the connection between corruption, being and seeming, *and* acting. First Hamlet accuses her of being 'like Niobe all tears' when following in the old king's funeral procession. Niobe was a mythological mother whose children died; she would not stop mourning and was turned to stone, still crying. In this thematic context, the use of a simile, '*like* Niobe', implies a performance – seeming, not being. Hamlet then observes that 'Ere yet the salt of her unrighteous tears/Had left the flushing in her galled eyes/She married'. Here the act of crying is seen by Hamlet as a metonymy for grief. But, moreover, in keeping with Hamlet's rejection of 'forms' above, it is merely an acted representation of grief, not grief itself.

Using the contexts of close reading to analyse Hamlet's soliloquy we learn through clear textual evidence that the 'that within which passes show' is not so much his grief at his father's death, but rather his disgust at his mother's actions – both in the sense of her *actual* behaviour and her *apparent* acting. These are the source of his despondency and the seed of the corruption that ruins his perspective on Elsinore. Though there isn't as much heightened language in the rest of the scene, there are still echoes of Hamlet's soliloquy in his conversation with his university friend, Horatio. When, for instance, Horatio tells Hamlet that 'I came to see your father's funeral', Hamlet responds with 'I prithee do not mock me fellow student,/I think it was to see my mother's wedding.' (1.2.175–177). Another thematic context that's picked up in the rest of the scene is being and seeming, with explicit reference to the ghost. Hamlet, not knowing that his father's shade has been spotted on the battlements of Elsinore, says 'methinks I see my father [... i]n my mind's eye' (1.2.183–184). Horatio has already used this same metaphor: 'A mote it is to trouble the mind's eye' (1.1.111). In both cases the *vehicle* is the eye, the *tenor* the mind, and the *ground* is the idea that the imagination or the memory *sees* the forms it conjures; in both Horatio's and Hamlet's case, what they are imagining seeing is Hamlet's father. Hamlet considers the possibility of the ghost in his own terms, namely as a sign of corruption, and the scene ends: 'My father's spirit – and in arms! All is not well;/I doubt some foul play [...] foul deeds will rise/Though all the earth o'erwelm them to men's eyes' (1.2.253–256), thus enabling us to interpret, in context, the last line of the scene.

SUMMARY: APPRECIATING THE WHOLE

The process of close reading outlined here, and using the three criteria of close reading (the crux, the relationship to the wider text, the relationship between the points of the analysis) opens up *Hamlet*'s words, lines, sentences, speeches and dialogues to some of their many and varied plausible readings. What it doesn't offer is closure: as though a careful re-reading will tell you *just what* the play means. It will tell you what it *can* mean, but each re-reading is likely to come to a different understanding. This is how texts last. It is why so few critics agree about the meanings of texts. It is an entirely – and endlessly – productive approach to literary study that can give almost all responsible readers the pleasure of their own idiosyncratic readings. This is not, of course, to say that 'anything goes'. Each close reading still needs to be rooted in the *language* of the play – the *words* on the page. But, as we have seen in this reading, there are so many variations in the meanings of those words, and in some cases different words altogether; so many ways the same words can be construed semantically, syntactically, and thematically; so many different types of cruxes that can be formed, that innumerable intelligent, diligent and appropriate readings can be discovered. Any extract from *Hamlet* can be appreciated in a similar way once a few core principles are understood, namely that *words only mean something in context*, and that this context may be understood **semantically, syntactically** and **thematically**, and, furthermore, that these contexts come together in **cruxes**. But, of course, these are not the only contexts. In the next chapter I will introduce one more: the **iterative context**.

FURTHER READING

S. S. Hussey. *The Literary Language of Shakespeare*. 2nd edn. London: Longman, 1992.

Frank Kermode. *Shakespeare's Language*. London: Penguin, 2000.

Caroline Spurgeon. *Shakespeare's Imagery and What It Tells Us*. Cambridge: Cambridge University Press, 1935.

John Dover Wilson. *What Happens in Hamlet?*Cambridge: Cambridge University Press, 1935.

5

THE ITERATIVE CONTEXT
PART 1: CHARACTER AND PLOT

At the end of Chapter 3, I presented a diagram of a re-reading cycle. What I hope you got from that was that any *part* of a literary work can only be properly understood in the light of the *whole*, and that each turn of the cycle enriches your reading experience. In the last chapter you saw how this works with the single word, 'green', which meant different things depending on how we related it to the larger structure of *Hamlet*. That is, the **semantic context** of 'green' was profoundly affected by the **thematic contexts** that we placed it in, each of which altered the tenor of the metaphor and thus the metaphor itself. This could be the court's fresh sense of grief; Claudius' knowledge of his inner jealously and guilt; or the play's, and in particular Hamlet's, harping on corruption. 'Green', then, formed what I called a **crux**. But the fuller meaning of the word – its ambiguities and possibilities – only become apparent once we have a sure sense of the play and the ways in which the play develops. My hope is that such an ambiguity brings with it a richer enjoyment of the language of the play; that complexity is, in itself, something that gives you as a reader pleasure – all the more so when you are equipped with the tools to unlock it.

1 REPETITION AND THE ITERATIVE CONTEXT

There is a clue in the reading cycle to the real secret of the pleasures of close reading – *repetition*. Repetition is a rather strange thing. It's something we often love – hearing the same piece of music over again, a regular beat that creates a rhythm in the body, re-watching a favourite film, eating the same foods, or re-reading a favourite book. Perhaps too often these are passive experiences, in that they are unexamined and make few demands of us; sometimes such pleasures become stale. It is also likely that you'll have something that you now love that you once didn't enjoy – that only persuasion, perseverance or a change in taste made a new and lasting favourite. These things we often love all the more and our attachments to them can be even stronger. Many important literary works fall into this latter category. There are a very few works of literature that have stood the test of time, or have been re-discovered and entered the canon, that do not, at least in part, resist easy absorption. Their most significant pleasures are, we might say, hard won. This can be for a number of reasons. The works could be written in an unfamiliar language (sometimes older, like Shakespeare's; sometimes fractured, like that of cummings) and as such their semantic and syntactic contexts are a challenge. They could be about things which are not, immediately, relevant to you as a reader. As such their thematic context is a challenge. I hope that I've begun to give you techniques to work through these initial moments of resistance.

Repetition, though, isn't just about your own good practice as a close reader. Repetition is also something that texts *do*. They repeat certain words – say, a name – and a character is born; they repeat ideas and images, and a theme is created; they are repeatedly interested in the consequences of an event, and a plot emerges. Without these repetitions narrative, as we know it and come to love it, could not happen. Sounds are also repeated; rhythms too. Structures on the page, like line lengths and stanzas recur again and again. These give us verse forms and poetry. Sometimes we expect a repetition and we don't get it. All literary rules can be broken to some intellectual or emotional end – disappointment, frustration, or the satisfying twist that reorganises all that came before.

Repetition, of course, is never (even when it looks like it) *just* repetition (recall Stein's 'Rose is a rose is a rose'). There are only twenty-six letters in the alphabet, but by placing them in different contexts we create countless words. Those words, many of which are repeated with a very high frequency, when placed in different contexts create numberless different meanings. This repetition with a difference is what I'm calling here the **iterative context**. To iterate is to repeat, but *with a difference*. It is iteration in this sense, rather than mere repetition, that creates lasting pleasure. In this chapter I'm going to introduce you to two ways in which this happens in narrative: *character* and *plot*; in the next chapter we shall look at two more: *sound* and *rhythm*. What is a 'character' but a certain set of words repeated in different settings? Character is consistent, or we won't recognise it; but also changes and develops, or we won't believe in it. What is a 'plot' but a set of iterations around a key event or events? If there wasn't repetition we wouldn't know we were reading the same story; if there wasn't variation, then there wouldn't be a story at all. Character and plot, then, are examples of the **iterative context**. We have, in fact, already seen another example, but one that is such a special case that it has a name of its own: the **thematic context**. A theme, like a character or a plot, is a *repeated form*; but, again like character and plot, each iteration will be slightly different. However, as themes are *so* important to the contexts of close reading we shall continue to think of the thematic context as a special case. Indeed, you will see that both character and plot, as iterative contexts for meaning, are intertwined not just with the thematic context, but also the semantic and syntactic contexts.

2 CHARACTER IN THE LIGHT OF THE WHOLE

What is a literary character? It's perhaps a good idea to begin with a question as fundamental as this. Certainly characters are one of the most important aspects of narrative – and one of the most enjoyable. It is characters – whatever they are – that very often draw us into, and make us persist with, reading. We care for them; we despise them; we are sometimes frustrated and even bored by them. They can evoke strong and lasting emotional responses. We, of course, work on the basic assumption that, as representations of people, characters are more or less like us; even while knowing quite well that they have no 'real' existence. Indeed, a literary character's only existence is a consequence of the imaginative work that we undertake when we see certain repeated ink marks on a page. We will usually start with the marks that we recognise as a name. Take, for example, 'Gatsby'. What does that *mean*? The question, rephrased for the methodology presented here, is 'what is Gatsby's **semantic context**?' An analogy would be with the word 'hobbit' at the outset of the story of that name. As we saw earlier, the word initially has *no* meaning; it accrues that meaning as we learn certain characteristics that become the context of that word's repetition (small, stout, hairy feet, clever fingers, silent, homely, brave, etc.). Names of characters work in a similar way. Initially they have no particular meaning beyond our unconscious predisposition to think that someone with a name will behave as – or at least be judged against – some minimal criteria of what it is to be sentient. These criteria involve, in large measure, an expectation of repetition: to be a character is to behave within a certain range of expected behaviours. Very obviously, with Gatsby, we get the iteration of particular verbal ticks – his 'old sport'; certain visual markers – his attractive smile; certain interests – his obsession with Daisy; certain settings – his glamourous parties (we looked at an example of this in some detail when thinking of the **syntactic context** in Chapter 3). Any character will have a greater or lesser number of these kinds of markers, as we shall see. They often become that character's through metonymy and synecdoche. For example, when there is a possessive pronoun – e.g. *his* smile; *his* party, *his* Rolls Royce. But what is important is that they *iterate* – not just repeat, but emerge in different contexts and thus reveal different aspects of that character.

Let's develop Gatsby's 'old sport' and think about its iterations within our re-reading cycle. From the outset it's intriguingly complex. Before we even get to meet Gatsby, there is a sense of mystery that creates the space for the name's semantic context, as the various party guests speculate on just *who* Gatsby is. 'Somebody told me they thought he killed a man', says one party guest; 'It's more that he was a German spy in the War', continues another (43). Then Nick starts talking to a stranger who he thinks he may recognise from his time in the army, and who invites him to go hydroplaning: 'Want to go with me, old sport?' (46). Glamour is there, metonymically, from the beginning, as the 'hydroplane' is associated with this phrase 'old sport'. But it only becomes significant for close reading purposes through iteration. Just a few turns of conversation later, after Gatsby has enlightened Nick about who he's talking to, he repeats the expression: 'I thought you knew, old sport. I'm afraid I'm not a very good host' (46). This time the phrase makes sure Nick knows that it's the speaker's (Gatsby's) party. So now the phrase is associated with Gatsby. It is, of course, not an *innocent* phrase. Nick recognises this almost immediately in the descriptive passage that follows. Here Nick creates an intriguing contrast between the Gatsby whose smile 'had a quality of eternal reassurance in it', that 'concentrated wholly on *you* with an irresistible prejudice in your favour', and someone 'whose elaborate formality of speech just missed being absurd. Sometime before he introduced himself I'd got a strong impression that he was picking his words with care' (46-47). The wider syntactic context here is decidedly ambivalent – both reassurance and mistrust.

As Gatsby leaves the scene to answer the phone shortly afterwards, he drops in the expression once again: 'If you want anything just ask for it, old sport' (47). It's repeated twice more before the end of the party. What we have now is the establishment of a literary character. A set of behaviours linked together by an iterated phrase. Our imagination has got something to hold onto, albeit just some words. We also have an attitude that is developing towards those words. Nick is clearly discomforted by their false sense of informality and assumed intimacy: 'The familiar expression held no more familiarity than the hand which reassuringly brushed my shoulder' (51). The semantic context of 'Gatsby' has begun to take shape, delivering what I called in the first chapter his **credible continuity**; but its syntactic context is both rich and complex because it is not neutral. Rather it contains the narrator's iterated judgement about Gatsby – the suspicion is that 'old sport' is a *learned* expression, one that is not natural to him or his upbringing, but is rather a line that is designed by Gatsby himself, to *create* a character. Indeed, the phrase is used by Gatsby forty-three times in the novel, implying its affected nature. The only time the expression is used by someone other than Gatsby is when Tom Buchanan, seeing through Gatsby's surface appearance, remarks

'All this "old sport" business. Where'd you pick that up?' (113). Tom recognises that Gatsby has learned the phrase – 'pick[ed it] up' – and that he is using it to hide something else.

COMPLEXITY CASE STUDY

Of course, this only makes sense in the context of the whole narrative, when we know that Jay Gatsby was once James Gatz. It fits, as a phrase, into a larger **thematic context** – the theme of 'appearance and reality'. Gatsby *appears* to be one thing, a charming, glamourous and wealthy man with an elusive but attractive back story; the novel reveals him in *reality* to be something else: a newly rich bootlegger who has risen from nowhere through luck and good looks. The phrase 'old sport' is integral to this thematic development, as well as to Gatsby's character. The semantic context of 'Gatsby', then, can be derived through the close reading of iterations. Not just the phrase 'old sport', but the way its iteration occurs along with other repeated associations. As we observed in Chapter 2, metonyms are a key way in which character is constructed. There, for example, the metonym 'New Haven' was used to associate Tom with Yale and all that goes with a high status institution. The equivalent with Gatsby is the repeated claim that his is an 'Oxford man'. When Gatsby tells Nick the concocted story of his life he says:

> I am the son of some wealthy people in the Middle West – all dead now. I was brought up in America but educated at Oxford, because all my ancestors have been educated there for many years. It is a family tradition.
>
> (60)

Oxford, and its prestige, is not just used to develop the idea of Gatsby, but also his family's firmly established cosmopolitan status. Again, and in line with the novel's thematic context, Nick is doubtful: 'He hurried the phrase "educated at Oxford", or swallowed it, or choked on it, as though it had bothered him before. And with this doubt, his whole statement fell to pieces' (60–61). The syntactic context provided for 'Oxford' by the narrator (swallowed, choked, doubt), with its implication that Gatsby is lying, generates our doubt. But Gatsby has a photograph of himself in 'Trinity Quad' wearing a blazer and holding a cricket bat, providing three metonyms that connote a firm place in the whole English class system, and that convinces Nick that 'it was all true' (62). Tom, again, sees through Gatsby: '"An Oxford man!" He was incredulous. "Like hell he is! He wears a pink suit"' (109). The clash between the metonymic vulgarity of Gatsby's pink suit and the cultured status that goes with 'Oxford' is too much for Tom. The narrative truth revealed by the whole, that Gatsby, was an army officer who went to Oxford for a few months after the war, is enough to convince both Nick and Tom that, in opposing ways, they are right about Gatsby; that their sense of his semantic context, what Gatsby *means*, is just what they think it is.

What we can see, in our close reading, is that 'old sport' and 'Oxford' become character **cruxes** for Gatsby, where more than one context of close reading is at work. Across the novel as a whole, Nick can hold onto his sense that 'there was something gorgeous about him' (8), and Tom's accurate conclusion that Gatsby is 'Mr Nobody from Nowhere' (115) is equally true. Gatsby's character, as it develops through the novel is constructed from the ambivalence that we can unearth when using the contexts of close reading.

3 PLOTTING A WHOLE

I want us to move away from *The Great Gatsby* and develop the iterative context further by seeing how it can be applied to another 'classic' novel, Emily Brontë's *Wuthering Heights* (1847). This time, rather than considering only character ticks, we'll think about iterations in the novel as a whole. Thus I have to begin with an assumption, namely that we have some sense of the **whole** of this novel and thus can choose appropriate parts of it for our purposes, such as a consistent thematic context and passages ripe for analysis. Of course, this isn't at all straightforward – *Wuthering Heights* is a complex novel, albeit very tightly woven together. A minimal plot outline runs as follows.

'Wuthering Heights' is an old house in the heart of the Yorkshire moors in the late eighteenth century. It is the family home of the Earnshaws. Mr Earnshaw returns from a trip to Liverpool and brings with him a young boy, Heathcliff, who had been abandoned and speaks only gibberish. Mr Earnshaw's children, who are about the same age as Heathcliff, have very different responses to him. Catherine becomes his inseparable companion. Hindley, her older brother, jealous of the attention his father and sister give to the orphan, becomes his bitter enemy. Mr Earnshaw dies and Heathcliff is left to the brutal treatment of Hindley. Heathcliff's own wildness and violence increase. As time passes the family come into contact with their rich neighbours, the Linton's at Thrushcross Grange. Edgar Linton, the son of the family, falls in love with Catherine and asks her to marry him. Heathcliff, believing that he can't compete, flees from the moors and isn't seen again for several years. When he returns Catherine and Edgar are married. Heathcliff has, mysteriously, become both rich and gentlemanly in the interim. He is still very much in love with Catherine and moves back into Wuthering Heights with Hindley. Hindley, who was briefly married and has a son, Hareton, is unable to get over his wife's death and has taken to drink and gambling. He sees the newly rich Heathcliff as a source of money and gets heavily into his debt. Edgar's younger sister Isabella is attracted to Heathcliff, who despises her as a Linton. Nevertheless, in order to revenge himself on Edgar, Heathcliff elopes with Isabella. They have a son, called Linton, but Isabella runs away from Heathcliff's cruelty before he is born and raises him away from the moors. Catherine, unable to bear the strain of Heathcliff's and Edgar's respective jealousies, and her overwhelming love for Heathcliff, goes mad, and shortly after she dies giving birth to Edgar's daughter, who is named Catherine in memory of her mother. Hindley drinks himself to death and, because of his gambling debts, Heathcliff takes over Wuthering Heights. When the second Catherine is about twelve, Isabella dies and a sickly and feeble Linton is returned to his father, Heathcliff, who hates him. But, in order to win the Linton estate and complete his revenge, Heathcliff tries to contrive it that the younger Catherine and Linton fall in love, eventually kidnapping her and forcing her to marry his despised and sickly son. Her father, Edgar, dies from a mixture of grief and ill-health and, as her father-in-law, Heathcliff takes over the second Catherine's inheritance, gaining possession of Thrushcross Grange. Linton and Catherine move to Wuthering Heights with Heathcliff and Hareton. Linton soon dies, and Catherine and Hareton, though at first hating and resenting each other, begin to fall in love; at the same time, and with his revenge almost complete – being in possession of both the Heights and Thrushcross Grange – Heathcliff unexpectedly loses interest in his plans and stops eating, acting as though all he can see is the ghost of the first Catherine. Heathcliff dies and Hareton Earnshaw takes back Wuthering Heights, the assumption being that he and the second Catherine will marry. These events take place between about 1770 and 1802, and we learn about them largely through the stories that the former eye-witness and housekeeper of the Heights, Nelly Dean, narrates to a man called Lockwood, who is renting Thrushcross Grange. Nelly's stories are framed by Lockwood's own eye-witness accounts.

One thing that emerges from my summary of this densely woven narrative is that the plot – more on which shortly – begins and ends with Heathcliff. His arrival at the Heights starts everything moving, his death at the end allows for resolution. This immediately directs us to his importance to the novel and may offer some grounds for selection of points of interest for our close reading, as the **cruxes** are likely to involve Heathcliff in some way. His character, then, will be important; but so will the themes that emerge along with it.

One place to begin, if we are to consider Heathcliff's character, is to take a look at his earliest description, when Mr Earnshaw returns from Liverpool. Such early descriptions of characters are always worth close attention, as they often establish key ideas that will be re-iterated. These iterations can usually only be discovered when re-reading; finding such patterns is often one of the most pleasurable parts of re-reading, as it leads to a mastery of the text. Nelly's narration of Heathcliff's arrival at the Heights runs as follows:

> We crowded round, and over Miss Cathy's head I had a peep at a dirty, ragged, black-haired child; big enough both to walk and talk: indeed, its face looked older than Catherine; yet when it was set on its feet, it only stared round, and repeated over and over again some gibberish that nobody could understand.

(25)

Now, on its own, this doesn't mean very much. But when we consider it **iteratively** it becomes interesting. Nelly's narrative description of Heathcliff would be surprising to a first reader, and of thematic interest to a re-reader, because even though *chronologically* this is our earliest view of Heathcliff, it is not his first appearance in the novel. That is narrated by Lockwood, and happens about thirty years later in time, but about twenty pages earlier in the story, when Lockwood leaves Thrushcross Grange and visits Heathcliff in the wild setting of the Heights:

> But Mr. Heathcliff forms a singular contrast to his abode and style of living. He is a dark-skinned gipsy in aspect, in dress and manners a gentleman: that is, as much a gentleman as many a country squire: rather slovenly, perhaps, yet not looking amiss with his negligence, because he has an erect and handsome figure; and rather morose.

> (3)

An attentive close reading, focusing on the **iterative context**, will show certain semantic continuities. For example the young Heathcliff is black-haired and wild, which is reiterated in the older Heathcliff's dark-skinned gypsy aspect; the younger Heathcliff is dirty, the older Heathcliff is slovenly. But there are also striking differences. The young Heathcliff is ragged, the older Heathcliff dresses like a gentlemen; the young Heathcliff cannot speak intelligibly and just stares around, the older Heathcliff is well-mannered and firmly in control of his comportment. Each of these semantic elements creates a different effect: the metonymies of dress provide discontinuous associations; the synecdoches of bearing are equally contrasting; whereas the synecdoches of colouring are continuous. The pronouns are also different: Nelly refers to an 'it'; Lockwood to a 'he'. It is the name – Heathcliff – that forces us, as readers, to put all of these elements, metonymies, synecdoches and pronouns, into the same semantic context.

If we are coming to this novel for the first time, we may find two things happen – our credulity is stretched and our interest is piqued. Is he a gypsy? Where does he come from? How does the ragged child become the upright and handsome figure? Is such a transformation reasonable? On re-reading, oddly, all of these questions become *more*, not less, mysterious. We still don't know where he comes from or how he was transformed. We have, as with Gatsby, a first person narration, and what our narrators Nelly and Lockwood don't know, we as readers don't know; but, unlike with *Gatsby*, there is no back story chapter such as the one that takes us from James Gatz to Jay Gatsby. Mystery and the identity of Heathcliff, then, becomes an obvious candidate for a **thematic context**. Not in the sense of actually *solving* the mystery, but in the sense of its persistence.

A brief passage from Nelly, speaking to Heathcliff of his possible pasts, creates a frame for this mystery:

> tell me whether you don't think yourself rather handsome? I'll tell you, I do. You're fit for a prince in disguise. Who knows but your father was Emperor of China, and your mother an Indian queen, each of them able to buy up with one week's income, Wuthering Heights and Thrushcross Grange together?
>
> (40)

Heathcliff's semantic context contains an essential gap. The thematic context of 'mystery' allows it to be filled in any number of different ways. But what this passage does is evoke a kind of inner nobility for Heathcliff: he's 'handsome', and 'fit for a prince in disguise', prompting the invention of a noble descent. These words imply a particular **generic context** (more on which in a couple of chapters): that of the fairy tale prince who's been mistaken for a pauper, but whose inner dignity cannot remain hidden, and whose real identity will be revealed at the end. A close reading of the iterative context of *Wuthering Heights* as it develops this theme, though, shows that this is not at all the case. Heathcliff is entirely self-made; his origins are never resolved. But Nelly's words tell Heathcliff what he will need to do to achieve that realisation of his *supposed* inner worth: 'buy up … Wuthering Heights and Thrushcross Grange'.

To create a compelling close reading, we need to attend to the parts of the novel's iterative context that can be seen to lead to this resolution – which, as related in the synopsis above, is exactly what happens (even if Heathcliff actually inherits by cunning rather than 'buy[s] up' the properties). This we can now do in brief. An analysis of three short passages will be enough. After Hindley's death, the Heights are found to be mortgaged to Heathcliff, and Nelly tells us that:

> The guest was now the master of Wuthering Heights: he held firm possession ... . In that manner Hareton, who should now be the first gentleman in the neighbourhood, was reduced to a state of complete dependence on his father's inveterate enemy; and lives in his own house as a servant.
>
> (136–137)

Here the key words are the inversions of 'guest' and 'master' that gives us Heathcliff's rise, and of 'first gentleman' and 'servant', that tells us of Hareton Earnshaw's fall. This is the first phase of Heathcliff's plan. The novel picks it up again when Linton Heathcliff, his son by Isabella, and thus a potential heir of Thrushcross Grange, is returned to him. Here he says to Nelly, then housekeeper of the Grange:

> my son is prospective owner of your place, and I should not wish him to die till I was certain of being his successor. Besides, he's *mine*, and I want the triumph of seeing *my* descendant fairly lord of their estates: my child hiring their children to till their fathers' land for wages.
>
> (151)

Here our close reading should note the iterated crux of inversion, the former servant's child hiring the children of his former master. Also the italicised possessive pronouns *mine* and *my*. Heathcliff wants to associate the estates with himself – to make them an aspect of his semantic context and fill out his name. Later, after Edgar's death, Heathcliff returns to Thrushcross grange:

> He made no ceremony of knocking, or announcing his name: he was master, and availed himself of the master's privilege to walk straight in, without saying a word ... It was the same room into which he had been ushered, as a guest, eighteen years before ... . Time had little altered his person either. There was the same man: his dark face rather sallower, and more composed, his frame a stone or two heavier, perhaps, and no other difference.
>
> (207)

This third iteration uses the inversion of master and guest as did the first. But it also makes sure that we, as readers, are aware that this is an iteration of Heathcliff. He's not identical, as that would be too fantastic after eighteen years. Iteration always comes with some small difference if character continuity is to be credible. The changes, though, are outward and carry through that darkness of skin that is a metonymy both for his lower gipsy status, but also his 'oriental' nobility: the ambivalence that makes his character's rise both believable and inevitable. He is, now, the 'first gentleman in the neighbourhood', by right and by bearing, but he also remains the wild child – the 'it' – that Mr Earnshaw brought back from Liverpool thirty years earlier.

4 PLACE: ITERATION AND RESOLUTION

Character and plot, then, can be understood using the **iterative context**; that is, by carefully pursuing the ways in which meaning accrues across the repetitions of a particular name or theme, allowing for growth while maintaining a credible continuity. Narratives, though, are not just about people. They also contain places and objects. These too can be understood iteratively. Places are often returned to in novels, but they are rarely the same – the relationship, for example, between the characters and that room or building will have changed. Heathcliff returning to the Heights and the Grange as guest and then master is a case in point, and both places could serve as cruxes. Objects can also take on a similar role. A place or an object is unlikely to be iterated as many times as a character in any particular narrative, but it can still resonate and be useful for interpreting a narrative as a whole.

An example, which will help you to see this more clearly, is the 'green light' that figures prominently in *The Great Gatsby*. The green light first appears at the end of the opening chapter. Nick is watching Gatsby, his neighbour, standing on the edge of his lawn in West Egg, looking over the bay toward East Egg: 'he stretched out his arms toward the dark water in a curious way, and, as far as I was from him, I could have sworn he was trembling. Involuntarily I glanced seaward – and distinguished nothing except a single green light, minute and far away, that might have been the end of a dock' (24). The syntactic context of this passage creates a sense of the green light's importance – Gatsby is 'trembling' and Nick is 'involuntarily' drawn to it. But its semantic and thematic contexts only become clear through iteration when Gatsby and Daisy have been reunited. Again, Gatsby is looking out over the water toward East Egg: "'If it wasn't for the mist we could see your home across the bay," said Gatsby. "You always have a green light that burns all night at the end of your dock'" (84). This second iteration creates the semantic context of the first: the green light is metonymically associated with Daisy, and so with Gatsby's aching desire for her. Now Gatsby's 'curious' gesture, and his 'trembling' makes sense when we re-read the first passage (even if Nick's response is less clear: the involuntary nature of his glance perhaps being a narrative necessity rather than a characteristic one – if Nick doesn't see the light, we don't).

The green light has become a **crux**, and we can see the thematic and semantic contexts overlapping. When opened up through this approach, Nick's comment on Gatsby's connection between the green light and Daisy enriches our whole reading experience:

> Daisy put her arm through his abruptly, but he seemed absorbed in what he had just said. Possibly it had occurred to him that the colossal significance of that light had now vanished forever. Compared to the great distance that had separated him from Daisy it had seemed very near to her, almost touching her. It had seemed as close as a star to the moon. Now it was again a green light on a dock. His count of enchanted objects had diminished by one.
>
> (84)

The language in the passage, the way it iterates the green light, marks its transformation, and a transformation of the theme of desire through the use of complex figurative language. The green light was, at first, a metonym for Daisy and as such charged with her absence. Daisy's presence, her physical contact (she puts her arm through his 'abruptly' – hardly a romantic gesture), can, for Nick, only diminish that desire. The simile he uses is wholly appropriate: 'It had seemed as close as a star to the moon.' The *tenor* is the relationship between Daisy and the green light. The *vehicle* is the closeness of the moon and a star. There is a pertinent ambiguity in the nature of the *ground*. Yes, looking up at the night sky (as Gatsby was just before Nick first sees him looking at the green light) the moon and a star are close together; but, in the reality of cosmic space they are light years apart. Closeness and distance – the markers of desire – are both reflected in the simile's ground. Closeness, in Nick's narration at least, suggests the transformation of desire, which is represented by the final metaphor: 'His count of enchanted objects had diminished by one.' The *tenor* here is the green light (and all it represented); the *vehicle* is disenchantment, the *ground* is the loss of something magical. Desire, it seems, is more important than attainment. To Nick, at least.

COMPLEXITY CASE STUDY

When looking at *Hamlet* in Chapter 4 the word 'green' also took on a rich and complex significance. There was Claudius' 'green' memory that was a figure (a metaphor and a metonymy) for freshness, corruption and jealously. In the immediate case above, green is a metonymy for Daisy. But in the wider novel 'green' also has the rich semantic context that it has in *Hamlet*. It figures both loss and desire – not just for Gatsby, but for America itself. For example, Nick uses the word as a metaphor for the wonder of the first settlers of East and West Egg: 'as the moon rose higher the inessential houses began to melt away until gradually I became aware of the old island here that flowered once for Dutch sailors' eyes – a fresh, green breast of the new world' (159). Here freshness and greenness are brought directly together and they spell the promise of the New World (the breast is also a metonym for the feeding of new life and innocence). But in the context of *The Great Gatsby* itself, which reeks of corruption like Hamlet's Elsinore, this green 'freshness' is ironically undermined. That first gaze upon a new promised-land has already begun to spoil it, just as Gatsby's desire-fuelled gaze at the light on Daisy's dock already contains the impossibility of that desire's fulfilment – as we shall see shortly.

5 ENDINGS AND ITERATIONS

Before drawing this chapter to a close I want you to think about a key tension that the iterative context throws up. If a novel ends then its iterations end; but if you are re-reading it then iteration becomes a part of a cycle. When, for example, you *re*-read *Wuthering Heights*, your interpretation of Lockwood's first encounter with Heathcliff is entirely different, as we know what lies under the gentlemanly surface. Each time you read it you will, very probably, have a different response as different elements resonate for you. There is, then, no end to reading; though there is an end to any particular novel. Even when a novel does end, that ending itself, just like its beginning, will be affected by *how* you have chosen to re-read the novel. Let's take the end of *The Great Gatsby* – certainly one of the most famous endings in all literature. Gatsby has been shot, Daisy and Tom have fled from Myrtle's death, and Nick is again looking out from the West Egg shore:

> And as I sat there brooding on the old, unknown world, I thought of Gatsby's wonder when he first picked out the green light at the end of Daisy's dock. He had come a long way to this blue lawn, and his dream must have seemed so close that he could hardly fail to grasp it. He did not know that it was already behind him, somewhere back in that vast obscurity beyond the city, where the dark fields of the republic rolled on under the night.
>
> Gatsby believed in the green light, the orgastic future that year by year recedes before us. It eluded us then, but that's no matter – tomorrow we will run faster, stretch out our arms farther .... And one fine morning –
>
> So we beat on, boats against the current, borne back ceaselessly into the past.
>
> (159)

This passage, with its strong thematic context of time, prompts us to read it cyclically; to find that frisson of pleasure in recognising a complex situation in which the past and the future are irrecoverably separate and yet totally intertwined. Of course the past is behind us and lost to all but memory, but even so it still defines our future actions. Gatsby's past is 'behind him', but he *believes* it to be in front of him. Not as something new or different, but as repetition. It is, though, that repetition that eludes us; the past, as Nick tells Gatsby, cannot be repeated:

> 'You can't repeat the past.'
> 'Can't repeat the past?' [Gatsby] cried incredulously. 'Why of course you can!'
> He looked around him wildly, as if the past were lurking here in the shadow of his house, just out of reach of his hand.

(99)

Gatsby's desire – his desire for the green light as a metonym for Daisy; his desire for Daisy herself, is about the recovery and repetition of something lost. A perfect moment. His life is tuned to that recovery; his self-invention is designed to live up to it. One past is the denial of another. Iteration, then, is both thematically and structurally crucial to *The Great Gatsby*. This is made evident by the contexts of close reading.

SUMMARY

Your own re-reading of any work, drawing on the iterative context, will allow you to understand the themes that matter, to master their complexity, to see how the elements that repeat with a difference across the whole of the that work enable it to hang together, even as they are shaping and being shaped by each part. Characters are a series of iterated elements that provide you with credible continuity. Plots are an iteration of events, or intertwined events, that relate to the developing theme of the work in question. Places are iterated spaces that can be left and returned to – but are never the same. Bilbo, returning to his seat by the fire transformed by his experiences at the end of *The Hobbit* is a crux that demonstrates all three iterative aspects combined: his character and sense of place has been transformed by the novel's plot.

FURTHER READING

H. Porter Abbot. *The Cambridge Introduction to Narrative*. Cambridge: Cambridge University Press, 2002.

Wayne C. Booth. *The Rhetoric of Fiction*. 2nd edn. London: Penguin, 1983.

Peter Brooks. *Reading for the Plot: Design and Intention in Narrative*. Cambridge MA: Harvard University Press, 1984.

Dorothy Van Ghent. *The English Novel: Form and Function*. New York: Harper and Row, 1953.

6

THE ITERATIVE CONTEXT
PART 2: SOUNDS AND RHYTHMS

The last line of *The Great Gatsby,* 'So we beat on, boats against the current, borne back ceaselessly into the past' (159), works as a complex and rich resolution to a novel, but it is also a call to re-read: to enter a cyclical relationship with the text that will deepen your reading experience. On the level of the whole, it summarises the vital thematic contexts of desire and time, loss and hope. But the line is open to an entirely different kind of interpretation. What happens if you change your focus of attention and *listen* to the line? Do you *hear* Nick's voice, do you *hear* the sounds of his words? If you do you'll notice that there are iterations in those sounds, continuing to take iteration as meaning repetition with a difference. The first sound you are likely to notice is the prominent 'b': 'So we **b**eat on, **b**oats against the current, **b**orne **b**ack ceaselessly into the past'. This, you'll remember, is called **alliteration**. If you continue to pay attention, you'll hear the 's/z' sounds: '**S**o we beat on, boat**s** again**st** the current, borne back **c**ea**s**ele**ss**ly into the pa**st**.' There are even more of these s/z sounds, but as, unlike alliteration, they are not at the front of the words, nor all even made by the same letter, this **sibilance** is harder to tune into. If you remain patient, you might notice the iterated 't' sounds too, and perhaps the vowel sound of the long 'e': 'So w<u>e</u> b<u>ea</u>t on, boats again**st** the curren**t**, borne back c<u>ea</u>selessl<u>y</u> in**t**o the pas**t**'. To alliteration and sibilance we can add **consonance**, the repetition of consonant sounds, and **assonance**, the repetition of vowel sounds. There is a density of sound in this line that, even given the finite nature of meaningful sounds we can utter, seems unusual. What, as close readers, do we do with these iterations?

1 SOUND, REPETITION AND ITERATION

The most important thing to recognise and to work with in your close reading is that *sound, on its own, doesn't mean anything*: it is too open. Sounds only *mean* when they are located in **semantic** and **syntactic contexts**, and you can only begin to use the iterative context of sound in your close reading practice when it is aligned with these basic contexts. **Thematic** and **iterative contexts** will add further weight. We can't, for example, just talk about 'b' sounds. This is a very common mistake. We often think that 'b' sounds are hard or harsh sounds because of words like 'bomb' and 'blast', but we can see this is not true when we think of words like 'baby' and 'bubble.' Sounds only *mean* when they are in a context. In the context of *Gatsby*'s last lines, you need to think about the way the iterated 'b' sounds set up a relationship between the semantic units *beat, boat, borne, back*. This relationship is actually quite clear − *beat* and *boat* are part of the extended metaphor of rowing that figures a movement forward through time (the *tenor* is moving through time; the *vehicle* is the boat rowed against the current; and the *ground* is the effort to move forward against something that is pulling you back). The other two 'b' words, *borne and back* complete the metaphor by figuring the failure to make progress against the pressure of the past. The iterative context of these sounds relates directly to the semantic context of the extended metaphor and the wider thematic context of the novel. In isolation, the 'b's are empty; in the contexts of close reading they are full. The 's' and 'e' and 't' sounds each work in a similar way, connecting words that have thematic and figurative ramifications: *we, beat, boat, against, current, ceaselessly, into*, and *past*. What this iterative reading gives us is an extraordinarily dense piece of prose, where almost every word works on more than one level, providing a series of integrated and overlapping **cruxes**. *Ceaselessly*, to take one example, fits thematically with the theme of cyclical repetition, also picking up on the sibilance of boa**t**s, again**s**t and pa**s**t. This is certainly not to ignore the sheer pleasure of the poetic euphony; it is, rather, to begin to understand why that euphony is not just a surface of sound, but is rather integral to the way the novel works.

We can see − or rather, hear − how sound and meaning are related to context by revisiting the expression 'silver-sweet' from

Romeo and Juliet. In response to hearing Juliet, Romeo exclaimed: 'How silver-sweet sound lovers' tongues by night,/Like softened music to attending ears' (2.2.165–166). Listening to this, the over-riding sound is sibilance: 'How **s**ilver-**s**weet **s**ound lover**s**' tongue**s** by night,/Like **s**ofte**s**t mu**s**ic to attending ear**s**'. Eight of fourteen words contain the sibilant s/z (one of them, twice). Each time they are either related to sound itself (silver, sound, tongues, music, ears, etc.), or to the speaker of that sound (lovers'). The thematic context that connects these iterations is the transformation of a voice by love – it becomes metaphorically 'silver-sweet,' and, through the simile, like 'music'. In the metaphor *silver* and *sweet* are words drawn from two other senses, sight and tastes, to figure a kind of bright and satisfying voice that fits the theme. However, iteration can also provide striking contrasts. Take the scene that comes towards the end of *Romeo and Juliet*, when a group of court musicians, who were supposed to have supplied the entertainment for Juliet's wedding to Paris, quarrel with the Capulet serving man Peter after her supposed death, and are about to come to blows:

> *Second Musician* Pray you put up your dagger and put out your wit.
> *Peter* Then have at you with my wit. I will dry-beat you
>   with an iron wit, and put up my iron dagger. Answer
>   me like men:
>   'When griping grief the heart doth wound,
>   And doleful dumps the mind oppress,
>   Then music with her silver sound'—
>   Why 'silver sound'? why 'music with her silver sound'?
>   What say you, Simon Catling?
> *First Musician* Marry, sir, because silver hath a sweet sound.
> *Peter* Prates. What say you, Hugh Rebeck?
> *Second Musician* I say 'silver sound,' because musicians sound for
>   silver.

$$(4.5.119–130)$$

In brief, the musicians don't want a fight, but instead to play with language – to exchange daggers for witticisms, weapons for words; and they combat using alliteration. Within this sound battle, Peter sets them a riddle: to explain the therapeutic value of music – and this is where Juliet's words are iterated – that is, its 'silver sound'.

But here 'silver hath a sweet sound' not because it is related to the theme of love, but, as the second musician points out, because of the tinkle of silver coins, in which the musicians hope to be paid. As the immediate syntactic context changes, so does the semantic context of the words *silver* and *sweet*. These words sound the same, but they mean completely different things. Context, again, determines the range of plausible meanings in our close reading; but the focus of that close reading is itself determined by iteration.

2 A SHORT POEM

When we think of paying attention to aspects of language like alliteration, assonance, consonance and sibilance we are usually thinking of close reading poetry. Though as you have seen with *Gatsby*, prose too will use these tools of meaning, poetry is the place where you should expect to be able to apply them with the greatest success. This is because poetry has long made an explicit virtue of using the full range of language's inherently iterative qualities. The following is a short poem by the English poet, Elizabeth Jennings:

'REMINISCENCE' (1953).

When I was happy alone, too young for love
Or to be loved in any but a way
Cloudless and gentle, I would find the day
Long as I wished its length or web to weave.

I did not know or could not know enough   5
To fret at thought or even try to whittle
A pattern from the shapeless stony stuff
That now confuses since I've grown too subtle.

I used the senses, did not seek to find
Something they could not touch, made numb with fear;   10
I felt the glittering landscape in the mind
And O was happy not to have it clear

The challenge, as always, is not just to relate the sounds to each other, but to find out their part in the whole. First, you need some kind of grasp of what the poem means, then you need to consider how sound may both create and intensify this meaning. That is, you need to work through the re-reading cycle. Luckily in this instance (though this is not always the case) the title gives you a clue as to the poem's meaning: 'Reminiscence'. In a very general sense, at least enough to give us a thematic context by which to make our choices of what iterations may matter, the poem's meaning can be outlined quite simply: when a child the speaker was solitary but content because they had a simple and direct experience of the world; now the speaker is older they have become anxious and fearful as the adult mind has come between them and the world. Of course, this simplicity is deceptive. A poet wouldn't write a poem if that was all that they had to say – so how do the poem's iterated poetic elements complicate and enrich this basic message?

One useful approach is to break the poem up into manageable parts. In this case we can think about syntactic units, that is, sentences, which here neatly coincide with the stanzas. What I'll present now is the first stanza with its basic sound iterations marked up, just as you could do quite easily by saying the poem out loud and writing on the text.

> When I was happy alone, too young for love
> Or to be loved in any but a way
> Cloudless and gentle, I would find the day
> Long as I wished its length or web to weave.

I have identified three sound iterations: 'w', 'l' and 'uh'. My basic criterion was at least three repetitions in two lines. The 'w' sound is consistently alliterative. The 'l' consonance is more various, coming at the beginning of words, or in the middle of words, and as both a clear 'l' (love) and a so-called dark 'l' (gentle); and even a silent 'l' (would), which I'm not counting here. The assonant 'uh' sound can be spelt in a variety of ways, such as ou (young), o (love), and u (but); but also the 'e' in 'cloudless' (cloudluss) in my English accent, at least, and the movement from t to l in gentle (gentul). So you need to attend to the sound not just to the eye in order to find it. Of course, as stressed above, there is no value in merely pointing out sounds. They need to be attached to words and meanings – that is, located in semantic, syntactic and thematic contexts.

In a very simple sense you could just focus on them one at a time, considering firstly how 'when', 'was', and 'would' relate to the past time, and then to the metaphor of the 'web' (the *tenor* is day; the *vehicle* is web; the *ground* is something both extended and strong); second, how 'alone', 'love', 'loved' form a surprising cluster. 'Love' and 'alone' would not normally go together – love is typically about being with someone else. But the point is that there are different kinds of love. Love in line 1, is adult, probably sexual, love. Love in line 2 is the love that a child gets from its family. They are connected through the iteration of the vowel and consonant sounds to 'young' and '*cl*oudless and gent*l*e'. The focus is on the *child's* sense of love. It is more interesting, then, when we begin to listen to the sounds as they interweave. In the last line of the stanza, 'I **w**ould find the day/*L*ong as I **w**ished its *l*ength or **w**eb to **w**eave.', the alliterated 'l' sounds in *long* and *length* overlap with the alliterated 'w' sounds in *wished, web* and *weave*, seeming, perhaps, to create the interconnections of the spider's web as they pick up the earlier iterations.

Each stanza opens up through this kind of detailed reading. In the second stanza, the prominent sounds are 'n', 't' and 's'. The 'n's in its first line are connected to knowing and negation – what was not known, which becomes what is known in the '**n**ow' of the last line. The 's' and 't' sounds can be seen in the extended metaphor '**t**ry to whi**tt**le/A pattern from the **sh**apele**ss st**ony **st**uff'. The *tenor* here is the adult life, the *vehicle* is failing to carve stone, and the *ground* is the resistance of something to shaping. The actual pattern of the words, their strength and organisation marked by alliteration and assonance, are in ironic conflict with the speaker's claim *not* to be able to shape their experience. The control of language is precise and effective – whatever the speaker may say. Perhaps this is one thing that poetry can do: give shape to shapeless experience. And, if you continue to pay attention to the sounds, you will hear how the last stanza picks up on the 'l's of the first and the 't's of the second, connecting them across a pattern of newly introduced sibilance. The limited sensual experience of childhood ('u**s**ed the **s**en**s**e**s**') is preferable to the questing after the transcendent ('**s**eek to find/**S**omething) because the senses of childhood are a '**gl**i**tt**ering **l**and**s**cape of the mind', where things are bright but not in focus, and all the more delightful for that.

Sound, then, is meaningful for close reading when you locate it in a **crux** – that is, when iteration brings words into alignment within a theme, or a metaphor, or some other context of signification. Assonance, alliteration, consonance and sibilance are not, though, the only sound based iterative contexts. Another important iterative form is **rhyme**. Of course, not all poems have a rhyme scheme, but Jennings' 'Reminiscence' does; even this is not to say that it necessarily matters. Rhyme, like the other sound patterns you have been listening for, only matters to a close reading when it is related to other contexts of close reading through the re-reading cycle. First, though, you still have to identify it. In this poem there is an *abba, cdcd, efef* pattern, where *a* and *d* are half-rhymes (love/weave; whittle/subtle), *b, c, e* and *f* are full rhymes. One thing you could look for is whether any of the rhyming words resonate with each other within the theme, or against it. Often half-rhymes are important. For example, the half-rhyme of 'love' and 'weave' suggests a lack of resolution and the end of the first stanza, avoiding the kind of conclusive end that would have been suitable if the poem had been about satisfaction rather than loss. As such, this iterated half-rhyme works within the thematic context. The actual resolving rhyme in the last stanza, fear/clear, is a full rhyme. But, the echo of 'fear' in the sound of 'clear' unsettles that clarity, suggesting that the adult anxieties have affected – perhaps even infected – the speaker's reminiscence. Again, the iteration in the rhyme is useful to our close reading when we see it as a crux.

3 A LONGER POEM

Tracing iterative patterns of sound is far from straightforward, but it is necessarily easier in a short poem than in a longer poem, where there are likely to be more of them. What is essential in close reading a longer poem, as with a longer novel or a verse drama, is to pick up on iterations that belong to the aspects of the poem which resonate with its thematic context. As such, the actual method is largely the same as with a shorter poem – the principal difference is that it will probably be more of a challenge to identify themes in longer work and there may even be a number of competing themes. Of course, the greater the challenge, the greater the pleasures of success.

The longer poem I want you to look at here is John Keats' 1819 'Ode to a Nightingale'.

My heart aches, and a drowsy numbness pains
My sense, as though of hemlock I had drunk,
Or emptied some dull opiate to the drains
One minute past, and Lethe-wards had sunk.
'Tis not through envy of thy happy lot,   5
But being too happy in thine happiness –
That thou, light-wingèd Dryad of the trees,
   In some melodious plot
Of beechen green, and shadows numberless,
Singest of summer in full-throated ease.   10

Oh for a draught of vintage that hath been
Cooled a long age in the deep-delvèd earth,
Tasting of Flora and the country green,
Dance, and Provençal song, and sunburnt mirth!
Oh, for a beaker full of the warm South,   15
Full of the true, the blushful Hippocrene,
With beaded bubbles winking at the brim,
   And purple-stainèd mouth;
That I might drink, and leave the world unseen,
And with thee fade away into the forest dim –   20

Fade far away, dissolve, and quite forget
What thou among the leaves hast never known,
The weariness, the fever, and the fret
Here, where men sit and hear each other groan;
Where palsy shakes a few, sad, last grey hairs,   25
Where youth grows pale, and spectre-thin, and dies;
Where but to think is to be full of sorrow
   And leaden-eyed despairs;
Where beauty cannot keep her lustrous eyes,
Or new Love pine at them beyond tomorrow.   30

Away! away! for I will fly to thee,
Not charioted by Bacchus and his pards,
But on the viewless wings of Poesy,
Though the dull brain perplexes and retards:
Already with thee! Tender is the night,   35
And haply the Queen-Moon is on her throne,
Clustered around by all her starry fays

But here there is no light,
Save what from heaven is with the breezes blown
Through verdurous glooms and winding mossy ways.   40

I cannot see what flowers are at my feet,
Nor what soft incense hangs upon the boughs,
But, in embalmèd darkness, guess each sweet
Wherewith the seasonable month endows
The grass, the thicket, and the fruit-tree wild –   45
White hawthorn, and the pastoral eglantine;
Fast-fading violets covered up in leaves;
      And mid-May's eldest child,
The coming musk-rose, full of dewy wine,
The murmurous haunt of flies on summer eves.   50

Darkling I listen; and, for many a time
I have been half in love with easeful Death,
Called him soft names in many a musèd rhyme,
To take into the air my quiet breath;
Now more than ever seems it rich to die,   55
To cease upon the midnight with no pain,
While thou art pouring forth thy soul abroad
      In such an ecstasy.
Still wouldst thou sing, and I have ears in vain –
To thy high requiem become a sod.   60

Thou wast not born for death, immortal Bird!
No hungry generations tread thee down;
The voice I hear this passing night was heard
In ancient days by emperor and clown:
Perhaps the self-same song that found a path   65
Through the sad heart of Ruth, when, sick for home,
She stood in tears amid the alien corn;
      The same that oft-times hath
Charmed magic casements, opening on the foam
Of perilous seas, in faery lands forlorn.   70

Forlorn! the very word is like a bell
To toll me back from thee to my sole self!
Adieu! the fancy cannot cheat so well
As she is famed to do, deceiving elf.

> Adieu! adieu! thy plaintive anthem fades   75
> Past the near meadows, over the still stream,
> Up the hill-side; and now 'tis buried deep
>   In the next valley-glades:
> Was it a vision, or a waking dream?
> Fled is that music ... Do I wake or sleep?   80

When approaching a poem like this, progress really should be slow. While there are effective *methods* for reading poetry, one of which I'm presenting in this book, there are no shortcuts. Certain iterative pleasures of this poem are, of course, there on the surface: they are in the immediacy of its sound. It needs to be read and re-read aloud, then the poetic effects of alliteration, assonance, sibilance, consonance and rhyme can be heard even if the words themselves, and the meanings they add up to, remain partially obscure. Of course, these sounds only have value for your close reading when you relate them to their semantic and syntactic contexts. You are more likely to choose the right words to investigate when you associate them in turn with the thematic context that emerges from the poem. This process is, once again, cyclical. You need to begin, then, with a theme – it may not be the only theme, but it will get you started.

The thematic context that I am, at first, going to use to frame my attention for the iteration of sounds is as follows: the contrast between a melancholy speaker and a joyous songbird. This is necessarily simplistic at this stage of our analysis. But it gives us a ground for selecting cruxes and building up a sense of the way the parts work to create the whole, and from that the theme itself can develop. In the analysis that follows I'm going to look at four cruxes, the first two in some detail. I shall begin with the first stanza, and, keeping it simple for now, focus on just one aspect of the iterative context, sibilance.

My heart aches, and a drowsy numbness pains	a
My sense, as though of hemlock I had drunk,	b
Or emptied some dull opiate to the drains	a
One minute past, and Lethe-wards had sunk.	b
'Tis not through envy of thy happy lot,	c 5
But being too happy in thine happiness –	d
That thou, light-wingèd Dryad of the trees,	e

In some melodious plot	c
Of beechen green, and shadows numberless,	d
Singest of summer in full throated ease.	e 10

The cluster of s/z sounds in the first four lines is obvious. But what draws together *aches, drowsy, numbness, pains, sense, as, some, drains, past, Lethe-wards*, and *sunk*? Each of these words is part of an extended simile 'as though …' The tenor is the speaker's pain, the vehicle is hemlock/opiate, and the ground is the state of unpleasant intoxication. Attention to the sound gives us an alternation of clean *s* and slurred *z* sounds which seem to mark this intoxicated state. This is pertinent to the thematic context of the melancholy speaker.

There are a couple of aspects worthy of further note. First, there is a paradox in the expression 'drowsy numbness pains/My sense'. Numbness is an absence of feeling; pain is an excess of feeling. This paradox is not unimportant for the theme, as 'pains' gives a sharpness and immediacy to the melancholy. It brings into focus for the reader what could otherwise be a rather diffused feeling. The sibilance also picks out the classical allusion which extends the metaphor of intoxication further at line 4. 'Lethe' (pronounced *leh-thay*) is a river in Hell. To drink from its waters brings forgetfulness. The punishment is that the damned cannot get close enough to benefit from its release. Again, then, the semantic context is paradoxical: the *ground* of the trope is that the speaker has availed himself of an impossible relief. Sibilance on its own, of course, doesn't deliver any of these meanings, but it does *focus the attention* of our close reading. This attention can also be pointed toward the last lines of the stanza, where the same sounds are iterated in the context of a liberated joy: the nightingale that: 'In some melodious plot/Of beechen green, and shadow's numberless,/Singest of summer in full throated ease'. The iterations work here by way of contrast, sharply distinguishing the bird's joy (singest, summer, ease) from the speaker's despair (drowsy numbness pains). You can see, then, both sides of the poem's theme – the melancholy speaker and the joyous bird.

This thematic context can be extended across the poem in a variety of ways. The second example I shall look at comes in the second and third stanzas. Here I will draw your attention to the f/v sound.

> That I might drink, and leave the world unseen,
> And with thee fade away into the forest dim –   20
>
> Fade far away, dissolve, and quite forget
> What thou among the leaves hast never known,
> The weariness, the fever, and the fret
> Here, where men sit and hear each other groan;

These iterations develop the melancholic sub-themes of intoxication and forgetfulness. The point being that the nightingale can only be heard. It is a disembodied voice for the speaker, lost in the forest. The repetition of 'fade' between 'leave' and 'dissolve' creates this yearning for disembodiment. The speaker's transformation would also enable him to 'leave' behind his material troubles – to 'forget' the 'fever and fret'. This is further reinforced by the play on words brought out by the iteration of 'leave' and 'leaves', the first is what the speaker want to *do*; the second is where, as the nightingale, the speaker wants to *be*. Rhyme also matters here. Forget/fret, known/groan both mark the speaker's distance from, and desire to be like, the nightingale. To forget what makes him fret, and to be like the nightingale which has 'never known' what makes men 'groan'. This is, then, very much about *sound* – the song of the bird against the groans of men; a disembodied voice released from the earth against the melancholic sound of the unhappy speaker. The theme with which we began is now enriched. The contrast is not just between man and bird, but between what they can create: birdsong and what in stanza four will be called 'the viewless wings of poesy' – where viewless means 'invisible' (*OED*). The aim of the speaker, then, is to become pure voice, the nightingale's song, emerging from the darkness of the forest, is the realization of this desire. It's no wonder that sound is so vital to this poem.

As the poem develops the speaker considers the cost of this disembodiment. The following stanza is complex, and I want us to pick out a few sounds (i, ee and eth), and the subtle repetitions and variations, that are used to expand the theme:

> Darkling I listen; and, for many a time
>   I have been half in love with *easeful* <u>Death</u>,
> Called him soft names in many a musèd rhyme,

> To take into the air my quiet <u>breath</u>;
> Now more than ever seems it rich to die,   55
>   To cease upon the midnight with no pain,
>   While thou art pouring forth thy soul abroad
>   In such an ecstasy.
>   Still wouldst thou sing, and I have ears in vain –
>   To thy high requiem become a sod.   60

The nightingale's 'full-throated ease' becomes here the speaker's 'easeful death'; the speaker's 'drowsy numbness pains' becomes his imagined end: 'To cease upon the midnight with no pain'. The half-rhyme – if it's even that – of 'die' and 'ecstasy' seems telling. Ecstasy should be a completion, but rather it is a further tension as the 'ee' sound of that word's 'y' (ecsta*s-ee*) is assonant with ease and cease. This awkward half-rhyme signals that the nightingale's ecstasy is not something the speaker can achieve – not in poetry and not in death.

The perfection of the bird's song is a fantasy; a window into a world imagined by the speaker:

> Charmed magic casements, opening on the foam
> Of perilous seas, in faery lands forlorn.
>
> Forlorn! the very word is like a bell
> To toll me back from thee to my sole self!

The *OED* tells us that 'forlorn' can mean lost, abandoned, wretched, desperate: all these aspects of its semantic context resonate equally within the theme. The sound of the word also resonates with many of those that surround it, iterating the 'f', the 'l', the 'r'. In particular, you might note that the 'l' of folorn makes an explicit connection to 'toll' and 'bell'; the bell-sound that, brings the f and l together, calling the speaker back to their 'sole se**lf**'. The alliteration and consonance here weaves a tight web, taking the focus of the poem back to the poet and away from the now lost nightingale. 'Forlorn', then, does not refer to a faery land, except in so far as it is a projection of the speaker. Indeed, the last lines of the poem brings the speaker back to earth, as the song of the bird retreats over the hills: 'Adieu! the **f**ancy cannot cheat so well/ As she is **f**amed to do, deceiving el**f**'. The re-iterated 'f's connect 'fancy' – a then current word for the imagination (*OED*) – with fame and 'elf', itself a full rhyme with 'self'. This marks the speaker's imaginative connection with the bird, which the speaker now recognises was a deception – a projection, perhaps, of their own forlorn feelings onto nature, which leaves them unsure of just what they experienced. They are, though, alone; the bird's music has 'fled'. But it can be traced and re-traced through the poem if you attend to its iterations in sound.

4 METRE MATTERS

Poetry makes use of repeated sound patterns, that is, it exaggerates and elaborates the natural limitations of language, namely that there are only so many sounds that can be understood in any particular tongue. It also makes use of – and exploits to its own ends – another aspect of language: rhythm. There is some kind of rhythm or stress pattern in all spoken language. But in poetry it often falls into traditional forms that have become settled through the centuries of the English language poetic tradition. These patterns, as repetitions, belong to the iterative context. In the technical language of literary criticism, these patterns are called **metre**; their classification and interpretation is **prosody**. There is an odd polarity here. From nursery rhymes to verse drama, one of the most pleasurable aspects of poetic language is its rhythm; but it is, without doubt, not only one of the hardest things to identify, it is also one of the hardest things to make work in a close reading. In this section I shall try to demonstrate some of the essentials for you.

Both the poems that I have been analysing in the last two sections, despite their differences in tone, diction, length, theme, and complexity, actually have the same underlying, or **frame metre**. If you go back a few pages and count the syllables in each line, you'll find that, typically, they add up to ten; you may also notice a repeated pattern of emphases. If you then carefully reread the first stanza of 'Reminiscence' and say the lines out loud, very slightly exaggerating the natural stresses, you should get something like this:

> When I was happy alone, too young for love
> Or to be loved in any but a way
> Cloudless and gentle, I would find the day
> Long as I wished its length or web to weave.

Here I've underlined the stressed syllables. For the most part, you'll see that they fall into an alternating pattern of an unstressed syllable followed by stressed syllable. But you'll also notice that it's not consistent. The mixture of regularity and irregularity is what is important for close reading. The regular aspect of these lines is called **iambic** pentameter. The 'iamb' is a two syllable **foot**, where the stress falls on the second syllable. Pentameter, where 'pent' is the Latin for five, means there are five of these feet in each line. This is the most common English metre. To make it a little clearer the lines can be rewritten as follows, which each foot marked off.

When I | was hap | py alone, | too young | for love
Or to | be loved | in an | y but | a way
Cloudless | and gen | tle, I | would find | the day
Long as | I wished | its length | or web | to weave.

There are, of course, some elements which don't seem to fit. For example, the first line has eleven syllables, with an extra syllable in the third foot. This would make it an **anapaest**, a foot with two unstressed syllables followed by a stressed syllable. This is a common **substitution**. Poets use substitutions for two main reasons: first, to move the reader's attention to certain points in the poem (the same reason they use other sound effects); second, to avoid the monotony of an overly regular rhythm. In this instance, we might notice that it focuses attention on that word 'alone', especially as the comma after 'alone' creates an extra pause in the line. This mid-line pause is called a **caesura**. This fits the thematic context of the poem, where the speaker wants to draw the reader to the unlikeliness of being both alone and happy.

Looking at the marked-up poem, you'll also notice that the last two lines begin with feet that seem to invert the iambic rhythm, as they are clearly stressed/unstressed: 'Cloudless', 'Long as'. This foot is called a **trochee** (pronounced *trow-key*). This is the most common substituted foot in iambic pentameter, and is very often used, as here, at the beginning of the line, again to shift the attention of the reader. Rather than taking the substitution on its own, it should always be put back into its immediate context: 'loved in any but a way/Cloudless and gentle'. We have already seen how the 'l' sounds pull 'love' into both 'cloudless' and 'gentle'. These words also seem to cut across the metre. '<u>Cloud</u>less' and '<u>gen</u>tle' are both trochaic words; their parallel falling rhythms suggesting the softness of their semantic context, seem to raise them above the frame metre, making them work together. Thus the metaphor 'cloudless' (the tenor is the way the speaker was loved when young; the vehicle is cloudless; the ground is clear, light, bright, warm) resonates with 'gentle', and their combined meaning stands out even more. The use of the trochee in '<u>Long</u> as' is simpler. By throwing the emphasis on the first syllable of the line, the line *sounds* lengthened. Compare '*Long as* I wished its length or web to weave' with '*As long* as I wished its length or web to weave'. This is called **mimetic syntax**, where the ordering of the words reflects what is being said, or form mimics content.

The frame metre in 'Reminiscence', then, is iambic pentameter; but it is the variations or substitutions which are primarily of interest in close reading. Another way in which the iterative pattern of the metre can become meaningful is the attention it throws onto line endings. The regularity of the metre always creates, in the mind, a small pause at the end of the line. Some poetry will use this to its advantage and coincide the punctuation with the end of the line (for example, the poetry typical of the eighteenth century). Jennings, though, avoids this throughout; rather her syntax continues across the end of the line. This is called **enjambment**. Its effect is often to create a less formal and more intimate poem, where metre and rhyme are less obvious, and thus their consequences are subtler. There is only one **end-stopped** line that is not the end of a stanza. Elsewhere the punctuation falls in the middle of the line, disturbing, as we have seen, the metre by creating caesurae. The one end-stopped line is line 10, the second line in the final stanza: 'I used the senses, did not seek to find/Something they could not touch, made numb with fear;/I felt …' Above I drew attention to the 's' sound here; the way they reflected the different experience of youth and adulthood. It is the adult 'fears' that are highlighted by the unique end-stopped line. The semi-colon is not a strong punctuation point, so the 'fear' and the 'felt' are still held together, sharply contrasting the adult numbness with the child's 'glittering landscape in the mind'. Such variations within repeated patterns are very often the aspects of a poem upon which a close reading can be built or further refined.

COMPLEXITY CASE STUDY

You can see all the same tricks in Keats' 'Ode': frame metre, metrical substitutions, caesurae, and enjambment. I've marked up the major metrical variations using italics below:

> That I might drink, and leave the world unseen,
> And with *thee fade* away into the for[*est dim* –]   20
>
> *Fade far* away, dissolve, and quite forget
> What thou among the leaves hast never known,
> The *weariness*, the fever, *and the fret*
> *Here, where* men sit and hear each other groan;

Line 20 has an extra foot (here bracketed), turning it into an **Alexandrine**. It's not, though, the final foot that's out of place, it is the second one, with two stressed syllables, called a **spondee**: 'thee fade'. Indeed, 'with', thee', and 'fade' all seem to have about the same emphasis. Spondees usually slow the reading, here bringing our focus onto the speaker's desire to be one with the disembodied bird. The next line echoes this spondee: 'Fade far'. The slow spondee, the alliteration, and the repetition of 'fade' even further emphasise the speaker's desire to become a disembodied song – or poem – that I discussed above. Line 23 is even stranger. It has only three stresses rather than five. The second foot of the line contains two unstressed syllables. This is called a **pyrrhic**. Pyrrhics usually have the opposite effect to a spondee, in that they speed the reader up, but this is defeated by the caesura, so there is a tension put on that word 'weariness' as it cuts against the metre and the natural reading voice. Later in that line the metre suggests that 'and' should be stressed ('**and** the **fret**'), but it would be forced rather than natural. Instead, the last syllable of 'fever' followed by the 'and' creates another spondee. This swift quietness focuses the reader's attention on the alliterated and metrically accented 'fever' and 'fret'. The enjambment between 'fret' and the trochaic opening on the next line, 'Here', followed immediately by a caesura, puts a lot of weight on that 'Here', bringing the reader firmly back from the flight of the birdsong to the pains of the speaker's earthly existence. Metre, then, works by variation and will often work with other sound effects to enrich the meanings – the themes – of the poem.

5 FREE VERSE

Because language itself is necessarily iterative, even poetry that doesn't have a frame metre – so-called **free verse** – will have some kind of rhythmic pattern. Often this comes from other forms of repetition, or from a more fragmented echo of traditional metre. A good example is a short poem by one of the pioneers of free verse, Walt Whitman, called 'A Noiseless Patient Spider', and published in this revised form in 1881:

> A noiseless patient spider,
> I mark'd where on a little promontory it stood isolated,
> Mark'd how to explore the vacant vast surrounding,
> It launch'd forth filament, filament, filament, out of itself,
> Ever unreeling them, ever tirelessly speeding them.   5
>
> And you O my soul where you stand,
> Surrounded, detached, in measureless oceans of space,
> Ceaselessly musing, venturing, throwing, seeking the spheres to
>   connect them,
> Till the bridge you will need be form'd, till the ductile anchor hold,
> Till the gossamer thread you fling catch somewhere, O my soul.   10
>   (377)

The first line of this poem is certainly rhythmical: 'A noiseless patient spider'. This could be three iambs, with the fourth truncated. Or you may hear the individual words as three trochees, ignoring the 'a', which would be taken as an **anacrusis** – there for sense rather than metre. Either way, a rhythm is set up. Only to be broken by 'I mark'd where on a little promontory it stood isolated'. This line begins with a suggestion of iambs, but there is no discernible metrical pattern after 'promontory'. The effect, then, is one of surprise and, perhaps, a renewed attention to other aspects of the language. 'Mark'd', for example, in lines 2 and 3, signifies the close attention the speaker is paying to the spider. Line 4 has strong repetition ('filament, filament, filament') as the spider creates its web. A web, of course, is made up of identical – or iterated – strands of silk. But the iterated word 'filament' also creates a stressed, unstressed, unstressed rhythm. This foot is called a **dactyl**. When this is noticed, suddenly a lot of the words in this poem are dactylic: 'tirelessly', 'measureless', 'ceaselessly', 'venturing', 'gossamer'. A dactyl has an accelerating rhythm that pushes the reader forwards, representing the spider's production of silk. Indeed, there are other dactyls that fit with this: 'Ever un | reeling them', 'speeding them', 'oceans of'; or that suggest dactyls: 'seeking the | spheres to con | nect', 'bridge you will | need be formed'. The poem never becomes dactylic, but it always carries with it the forward thrust offered by that metre which here is connected with the spider's spinning. This spider's spinning, when we consider the **thematic context**, is not important in itself, but in the second stanza becomes an extended metaphor for the lonely speaker's soul's attempt to attach itself to the world. The *tenor* is the soul's attempt to overcome its isolation; the *vehicle* is the spider attaching its web across a void; the *ground* is a small thing creating connections across a vast space. The dactylic cadence, then, becomes mimetic of the urgency of the speaker's need for attachment. Rhythm, then, as an aspect of the iterative context, can still be part a key part of the close reading of a poem which, on the surface, appears not to have any specific iterative qualities.

SUMMARY

Sound is one of the most alluring and pleasing elements of poetry, and it also does its work in prose. Sound without context, though, is meaningless for us. In our close reading practice we need to relate it to one or more contexts. The iterative context is primary here as it calls our attention to clusters of sounds which are in excess of normal usage, through assonance, consonance, etc., or through rhyme and metre. These clusters become important for our critical interpretations when they form cruxes with other contexts of close reading, and thus draw us to reflect on the thematic, semantic, and syntactic contexts. These cruxes are undoubtedly amongst the most highly complex achievements of literary language; but they use one of language's simplest pleasures: the repetition of sound.

FURTHER READING

Philip Hobsbaum. *Metre, Rhythm and Verse Form*. London: Routledge, 1996.

Robert Pinksy. *The Sounds of Poetry: A Brief Guide*. New York: Farrar, Strauss and Giroux, 1998.

John Strachen and Richard Terry. *Poetry*. Edinburgh: Edinburgh University Press, 2000.

7

THE GENERIC CONTEXT

Looking back at the e. e. cummings poem, 'since feeling is first', you'll remember that it was only when we recognised its **genre**, namely that it was a *carpe diem* poem (about 'seizing the moment') that it began to make sense. The genre focused the complex semantic and syntactic contexts by giving us set of conventions from which we could deduce a theme. That is, we used the poem's **generic context** to work out its meaning. We have been using generic contexts, sometimes explicitly, sometimes quite unconsciously, to shape meanings throughout this book, from *The Hobbit's* *fantasy* dwarves and dragons, to Romeo and Juliet's *romance*; from Heathcliff's *realist* continuity of character, to Hamlet's *tragic* brooding melancholy.

Each time you have engaged with a particular text, you have perhaps unwittingly drawn on your reading expertise to recognise the ways in which *what* you are reading, its genre, shapes *how* you can read it. The familiarity of conventions is central to the enjoyment of literature. This is because it matters whether your expectations are met (or exceeded or challenged), and also because you will often choose what you read according to the genres you like. Likewise, reading outside of your generic comfort zone (e.g. cummings' modernism) brings with it significant challenges. It has, though, rarely been obvious that this is what has been going on. In this chapter we shall reflect more deeply on genre, and consider the ways in which the generic context plays its part in our developing practice of close reading; in particular the ways in which a conscious sense of the generic context of what we are reading changes the mode of attention and controls and constrains the semantic, syntactic, thematic, and iterative contexts.

1 MAGIC AND THE GENERIC CONTEXT

Take, for example, the following phrase used to describe hobbits that was referred to in Chapter 1: 'There is little or no magic about them, except the ordinary everyday sort which helps them to disappear quietly and quickly when large stupid folk like you and me come blundering along' (12). If we know we are in the 'fantasy' genre, then the semantic context of 'magic' is literal, and we will conclude that hobbits have some, albeit small, supernatural ability. We have quickly located ourselves in a world where what is 'ordinary' is very different from what would normally be considered ordinary. By way of contrast, take this description of Daisy's singing voice from *The Great Gatsby*: 'When the melody rose, her voice broke up sweetly, following it, in a way contralto voices have, and each change tipped out a little of her warm human magic upon the air' (97). Here we don't believe that Daisy has any supernatural power. As such, the semantic context of 'magic' is metaphorical: the *tenor* is Daisy's voice; the *vehicle* is 'warm human magic'; and the *ground* is the way things can affect us in a powerful and inexplicable way. Metaphors of magic and enchantment are strewn throughout *Gatsby*. But because we know that the world is a 'real' world, we treat them exclusively as figurative. If Daisy was an elf singing in Middle-Earth, we would construe the sentence quite differently. The **generic context** of the type of book we are reading, then, controls and often limits the semantic and syntactic contexts of words.

2 THE SONNET

You may think that the more rigid the conventions of the generic context the less opportunity there is for creativity and variation. Counterintuitively, this turns out not to be the case. A good analogy is with sport. All sports have strict rules, which are the equivalent of generic conventions, but not only are no two sporting matches identical, there is actually a huge range of possible plays that allows for – indeed, demands – indefinite creativity within the rules. Constraint is, arguably, a *condition* for creativity, rather than a check on it. Perhaps the most rule bound, or conventional, literary genre is the poetic genre of the sonnet; yet poets have experimented with the form for over 500 years, using its flexible generic context in countless ways.

The sonnet has a very specific set of traditional conventions. These can be summarised as follows (you'll find this sort of information in most good dictionaries of literary terms – see further reading):

- Fourteen lines.
- Frame metre of iambic pentameter.
- A rhyme scheme that creates one of the following patterns:
  - Two quatrains (four-line stanzas) and a sestet (six-line stanza) e.g. *abba cddc efggfe*. This is often called a Petrarchan or Italian sonnet.
  - Three quatrains and a couplet, e.g. *abba cddc effe gg*. This is often called a Shakespearean or English sonnet.
- The theme is traditionally love.
- The theme is presented, more or less explicitly, as a developing argument (e.g., thesis, antithesis, synthesis).
- The theme is expressed through figurative language and dense syntax.
- A *volta*, or 'turn', that marks a shift in the argument – usually at line 9, but sometimes at line 12.

What poets have done is taken these basic conventions and exploited their potential variations. The frame metre can contain iterative variations to shift your focus around the words. The rhyme scheme can be offset by half-rhymes, or re-ordered in a wide variety of ways that preserve or slightly disorder the stanzaic structure. The theme is probably the convention that is most often varied. Though originally sonnets were about romantic love, and in particular about a man's love for an elusive and beautiful woman, they have been used, at least since the sixteenth century, to frame other kinds of love: platonic, familial, and religious; and since the Romantic period sonnets' themes have been opened up to the political and the artistic.

What has been consistently the case, though, is that the sonnet's form, the generic context it creates, is used by poets to create a particular density of complex meaning that relies on the understanding of the form's conventions. As close readers we need to be aware of these conventions as they will shape our interpretations. We can see how this works through the example of Elizabeth Barrett Browning's 'Sonnet XIII' from her sequence *Sonnets from the Portuguese* (1846/1850):

> And wilt thou have me fashion into speech
> The love I bear thee, finding words enough,
> And hold the torch out, while the winds are rough
> Between our faces, to cast light on each?—
> I drop it at thy feet. I cannot teach   5
> My hand to hold my spirit so far off
> From myself...me...that I should bring thee proof,
> In words, of love hid in me out of reach.
> Nay, let the silence of my womanhood
> Commend my woman-love to thy belief,—   10
> And that I stand unwon, however wooed,
> And rend the garment of my life, in brief,
> By a most dauntless, voiceless fortitude,
> Lest one touch of this heart convey its grief.
>
> > (Barrett Browning, Forster ed. 222)

The work's **generic context**, as a sonnet, will be our starting point. First, there is the rhyme scheme: this is abba abba cdcdcd (admittedly there are a few half rhymes: rough/proof/off; hood/wooed). When split into repeating units it gives us two 'abba' **quatrains** and a six line 'cdcdcd' **sestet**. This is a Petrarchan form. This also fits the punctuation of the poem, with sentences ending at lines 4, 8 and 14. We can, then, using its generic context, think of the poem structurally as two quatrains and a sestet, each giving us a syntactic contextual unit, and analyse it accordingly by beginning with the first quatrain, as long as we remember to put it altogether again before the end.

QUATRAIN 1

> And wilt thou have me fashion into speech
> The love I bear thee, finding words enough,
> And hold the torch out, while the winds are rough
> Between our faces, to cast light on each?—

This first quatrain, as noted, is a single sentence. It dramatises the face-to-face confrontation of two lovers; which fits the broad thematic context of the sonnet tradition. In order to think about it semantically and syntactically, we need to break it down into its units of meaning, that is, into its clauses. The first clause runs: 'And wilt thou have me fashion into speech/The love I bear thee'. The question implies the setting of an ongoing encounter, as beginning with 'and' suggests these lines are following on from something prior, and the 'wilt', implies that the speaker has been in some way asked to create language that will express ('fashion into speech') the love they feel for the addressee. The next clause extends this, and to 'fashion in to speech' becomes a question of 'finding words enough'. Does this mean 'enough' in the sense of number of words, or of words that can contain enough meaning? In the poem the semantic context is ambiguous. These first two lines, then, establish that the speaker is a lover who has been asked to find the words to express their love. In addition, the archaic diction ('wilt', 'thee', 'thou'), in anachronistically echoing the language of the English Renaissance, locates this poem even more firmly in the tradition of the sonnet as love poem.

In lines 3 and 4 the poem becomes more complex: 'And hold the torch out, while the winds are rough/Between our faces, to cast light on each'. Here we may usefully go in a bit deeper. What emerges in these lines is the intense image of two lovers, faces close together, illuminated by a flickering torch, one trying to articulate a love demanded by the other. The picture this appears to create, though, is developed in quite a different way. In terms of the syntax we get the 'torch' held out first, and we have to locate this word 'torch' in its syntactic context and see it as a flame. We then get the 'rough' winds which will cause the flame to flicker, creating dramatic and moving reddish light. The wind is rough 'between' the faces which are then revealed in this unsteady flame-light.

The language is complex (sonnets, typically, are linguistically dense, and as such this is a generic expectation) and we need to think about how this image hangs together with the first two lines. What is the syntactic connection between 'fashion[ing]' words into speech that will disclose a lover's feelings and a 'torch', 'rough winds', 'light' and 'faces'? In terms of the drama of the situation, should we take this to be literal? Namely, that these two people really stood there in the torch light examining each other's faces, reaching for words to express their love. It seems to me unlikely (though not impossible). As such these lines are almost certainly worth exploring as figurative. It's not a torch or winds but something they represent that will help us to understand this dramatic situation. One way to get into it might be to consider the iterative parallelism between lines 1 and 2 and lines 3 and 4 suggested by the fact that both sets of lines begin with 'And' followed by a similar (if not quite identical) syntax. This iteration would imply an analogy between *words* and *torch light*, and thus between the difficulty of expression and the difficulty of clear illumination. As such the metaphor can be unpacked as follows: the *tenor* is the expression of love; *vehicle* is the flickering light; and the *ground* is something unsteady, inconstant – something that won't stay still. The reading seems to be: just as words are not stable enough to reveal my true feelings of love, the torchlight is too unstable to reveal our true faces. The conventional metaphor of understanding equalling clear sight underlies this poetic innovation (e.g. 'I see what you mean'). In each case a clear representation, of feeling and of self, is made difficult by either the limitations of language or by whatever it is that the 'rough winds' represent: perhaps passion; perhaps an argument. Whatever it is, it has complicated the context of the lovers' conversation.

That's just the first four lines, and I hardly feel I've completely conquered them. But looking at the metaphors and the sentence structure (the semantic and syntactic contexts) has certainly helped to begin to get a sense of the problem the sonnet is dealing with, that is, its thematic context, which is really given us by our expectations of the generic context of the sonnet. And, I suppose, it shouldn't be a surprise that when a poem is suggesting that expression is difficult it will, itself, be difficult (as with cummings in Chapter 3). The sonnet is trying to find a set of images to represent something that the sonnet itself implies cannot be represented. Now, one thing we know is that in a sonnet the theme, or argument, will be developed across the whole. As such, when looking at the next four lines, rather than beginning again, we can look to see in what ways they pick up the established theme.

QUATRAIN 2

I drop it at thy feet. I cannot teach   5
My hand to hold my spirit so far off

From myself...me...that I should bring thee proof,
In words, of love hid in me out of reach.

In many ways this seems like a restatement of the problem. If we take the 'it' of the short sentence that begins line 5 to be the 'torch' of the first quatrain, then, recalling the connection between the light and words, the speaker of the poem is refusing even to attempt to represent her relationship to her lover. It's also at this point that we get a real clue as to what the torch is trying to figure: it is the speaker's 'spirit'; that is, the speaker's deepest self. We can use this to reflect on the first quatrain. Language and light, now, are *vehicles* to represent the *tenor* which is the deepest self. The *ground* of this metaphor is, then, the self as something linguistically unstable; a self whose language is endangered by the metaphorical rough winds of the encounter. That self, in this quatrain, is dropped at the lover's feet. But the image is then withdrawn by the speaker, as though this attempt at an expression was a failed thought experiment – actually the speaker *can't* hold their 'spirit so far off/From myself...me'. It is, then, as though the first part never happened; the attempt at communication broke down and needs to be restarted. The iteration of 'myself' and 'me', held together by that enigmatic ellipsis ('...') suggest the speaker wrestling with a kind of doubt that leads to a further breakdown in expression reflected in the **mimetic syntax**. In the last two lines we return to the beginning of the sonnet: that any verbal 'proof' of the speaker's love is impossible because too deeply 'hid in me out of reach'; too much a part of that self which cannot be revealed as either light or language.

SESTET

Nay, let the silence of my womanhood
Commend my woman-love to thy belief,—   10
And that I stand unwon, however wooed,
And rend the garment of my life, in brief,
By a most dauntless, voiceless fortitude,
Lest one touch of this heart convey its grief.

The sestet begins with a 'nay'. After two false starts the earlier quatrains are both denied. In a sonnet line nine often contains the **volta** – after the Italian word for 'turn', where the argument of the sonnet shifts. This sonnet exemplifies just such a *volta* as we move from attempts at expression to seeing what silence can do. 'Silence', if we just take it as a contextless word, has a variety of possible meanings: it can be a request or an order; it can be a state of the world or the choice of person, it can be something we welcome, or something that ostracises us, amongst other things. What, then, does 'the silence of my womanhood' mean? 'Womanhood' itself is a pretty unusual word (unlike the more common 'manhood'). If we take it to mean 'the quality of being a woman' then how does this affect the meaning of silence? Is it her womanhood itself that is silent or is she silent because of her womanhood? What is the connection between womanhood and silence? (The nature of this as a 'Victorian' problem, rather than a semantic problem, is something I'll return to in the next chapter when we deploy the **adversarial context** to explore this son-net's history and relation to an individual's biography). It cer-tainly seems to be a valued kind of silence; for if words are not enough then silence may be. The point is perhaps that her lover can have belief in her 'woman-love' only because she has *not* spoken it – just as 'faith' in a silent God is often reinforced rather than weakened by that God's silence. The lover, then will have faith in her, and understand her faith in him, only if she is silent. The speaker's silence (and the irony of that will be touched on shortly) becomes then a kind of victory – she is 'wooed' but 'unwon'. This might hint at an intact virginity; certainly at some kind of restraint beyond the restraint of language alone (here ideas of 'womanhood' and 'girlhood' might come into play).

The next lines tell us that though she stands 'unwon' it's hardly a peaceful victory, as she is 'rend[ing] the garment of [her] life [...]/By a most dauntless, voiceless fortitude'. It is taking all the speaker's effort to remain silent; it is a brave ('dauntless') and stoic ('fortitude') silence that tears this garment. What 'the garment of my life' represents is, I think, extremely ambiguous. The rending of clothes has an unmistakably violent sexual connotation. But here it seems to figure the opposite of that – being rent because you *don't* give in rather than because you *do*. Perhaps the garment of her life is, rather, her body itself, the desires of which stand in opposition to her spirit (the *tenor* is body; the *vehicle* is garment; and the *ground* is that which is only worn over the essential self, that is, the spirit). The rending is the damage done to a body by silencing, and thus repressing, a feeling. But, the rest of the sonnet tells us, this repression is, itself, protective at a deeper level, because what the speaker seems to fear above all is what's given by the last word of the poem: 'grief'. An unspoken love, like faith itself, cannot be broken. Revelation, however, could lead to a crushing disappointment – be it either rejection or consummation. The deeper irony, though, is that all this is written down and thus presented to the lover. The speaker is fully exposed, and the very denial that a passion or a love – or both – cannot, or better, ought not, to be spoken is itself denied by the existence of the poem.

Thought together, the two quatrains and the sestet create a kind of progression: first, love *cannot* be spoken, second, it *will* not be spoken, and third, it *should* not be spoken. Put altogether this exists in tension with the very existence of the whole poem. The question then remains is whether the poem is a successful attempt to express the inexpressible or a failed attempt to remain silent. I won't attempt to answer that here. I'm not sure that I can.

Again, there's no way that all elements of this poem have been considered (I've not looked, for example, at sound patterns, which belong to the poem's **iterative context**), but a detailed reading has been made available by thinking about the way that we can use the **generic context** to order our interpretation of the different parts of the poem, that is its **semantic** and **syntactic context**, comprised of lines, sentences, quatrains and sestets, picking up on patterns of metaphor and the images they provoke within a coherent exploration of the **thematic context**: poetry's necessary failure to express love. A re-reading of this poem now, with this fuller understanding, should certainly be more pleasurable than a first reading merely because of this interpretative power.

COMPLEXITY CASE STUDY

You may well have thought that this poem of just fourteen lines was complicated enough and that even the quite extensive reading offered here, at well over 2,000 words, was plenty. I wish it were that simple. What makes things a little more difficult for the advanced reader is that this poem exists in at least two forms. There is an 1846 manuscript version which sits in the British Library. In the following I've indicated the differences from the 1850 version we've just looked at by striking through the words that were changed or omitted in the published version and putting the original words in bold type. There are also a few minor changes to the punctuation, such as the idiosyncratic use of two dots for an ellipsis.

> And wilt thou have me fashion into speech
> The love I bear thee, finding words enough,
> And hold the torch out, while the ~~winds~~ **words** are rough,
> Between our faces, to cast light on each?. .
> I drop it at thy feet – I cannot teach   5
> My hand to hold my spirit so far off
> From myself . . me . . that I should bring thee proof,
> In words . . of love hid in me out of reach.
> Nay, – let the silence of my womanhood
> Commend my woman-love to thy belief, –   10
> And seeing that I stand unwon, however wooed,
> ~~And rend~~ **Rending** the garment of my life, in brief,
> By a most dauntless, voiceless fortitude,
> Lest one touch of this heart, convey its grief.
> > (After Barrett Browning in Bolton and Holloway eds, 383)

In this complexity case study, I shall analyse only one of these changes: the difference between the 1850 version's 'rough *winds*' and 1846 version's 'rough *words*'. Plugging rough 'words' back into the first quatrain changes the initial context of the encounter of the speaker and the lover into an ongoing argument. The challenge of 'finding *words* enough' comes now from the heat of the confrontation. Also, the word 'rough' becomes the metaphor (albeit a very dead one) rather than 'rough winds' figuring a dramatic confrontation. This change also completely alters the way the 'torch' image works as there is no longer a rough wind to create the flickering light that created such a powerful meta-phor for the troubled expression for the speaker's love. In the 1846 version the torch light is much clearer, as are the faces. It may be that there are more subtle readings available, but it appears to me that changing 'rough *winds*' to 'rough *words*' nar-rows the ambiguity and thus the range of meanings the reader can enjoy. As such I think we can see why the amendment was made. 'Winds' creates a more dynamic and dramatic effect than 'words' because it is less explicit, and we can understand this by thinking carefully about the ways words work in semantic, syntactic, thematic and generic contexts.

3 TRAGEDY

Though the poetic genre of the sonnet has been around at least since fourteenth-century Italy, and in the English tradition since the sixteenth century, some literary genres are considerably older. Tragedy, for example, has existed since the fifth century BC. The resistance to change of generic conventions is, of course, the principal reason why a literary form like tragedy can recognisably exist for over 2,000 years. But flexibility within any genre is just as important. Simple repetition, as we noted with the iterative context, can be deadening; but iteration – repetition with a difference – is very often keenly pleasurable. What is of interest to both writer and critic is the extent to which genres, like the sonnet or tragedy, can be rigidly reinforced or adapted around the edges. In either case, the generic context will empower interpretation. Tragedy, though, over the centuries has not just been played with, it has actually evolved into a variety of different forms. Two of these are of interest to us here, and both stem from the classical world: Greek Tragedy and Revenge Tragedy. The conventions of these sub-genres of tragedy can provide different generic contexts by which to interpret a single text, in this case Shakespeare's *Hamlet*. If I tabulate, albeit in a brief form, the main generic conventions of each of these sub-genres you'll begin to see that both can be applied to *Hamlet* (as above, good dictionaries of literary terms will usually be able to provide these conventions – see Further Reading):

CONVENTIONS OF REVENGE TRAGEDY

a   *Corrupt social milieu*: Disordered, immoral and flawed society.
b   *Injustice*: As source of corruption, creating a wronged hero for whom the legal system fails to give justice.

c   *The avenger*: A highly flawed individual, who is either mad or feigns madness, who is initially hesitant to act and uses duplicity and deception as strategies.

d   *Revenge and retribution*: Complex overlapping plotlines, leading to extensive suffering.

e   *Violence*: Blood, spectacle and death; high levels of emotional passion.

f   *Restoration*: A legitimate a stable order is restored, but at the cost of the avenger's life.

(After Stanners 13)

CONVENTIONS OF GREEK TRAGEDY

a   *Harmartia*: Gk. 'error'; tragic flaw or error of judgment.

b   *Hubris*: Gk. 'insolence, pride'; the self-indulgent confidence that causes a tragic hero to ignore the decrees and warnings of the gods, and through his defiance bring about his downfall.

c   *Anagnorisis*: Gk. 'recognition'; the moment when the truth is discovered by the 'hero'.

d   *Peripeteia*: Gk. 'sudden change'; the reversal of the hero's fortunes.

e   *Nemesis*: Gk. 'retribution'; the fate that overtakes the tragic hero.

f   *Catharsis*: Gk. 'purgation'; the pity and terror evoked by the tragedy's resolution.

In many respects *Hamlet* is a prototypical revenge tragedy. Each of the revenge tragedy conventions would be fairly easy to map onto the play, providing a guiding generic context for key elements of its meaning. Hamlet announces himself as a revenge hero in the first act. Before his father (the ghost) has even revealed his murderer, Hamlet says: 'Haste me to know't that I with wings as swift/As meditation or the thoughts of love/May sweep to my revenge' (1.5.28–30). If we make the decision to see this play as a revenge tragedy, though, certain elements of complexity that we have found in our close reading may be disqualified. Take, for example, the lines from Hamlet's first soliloquy that we looked at as a **crux** in the Case Study:

> O God, God,
> How weary, stale, flat, and unprofitable
> Seem to me all the uses of this world!
> Fie on't, ah, fie, 'tis an unweeded garden   135
> That grows to seed, things rank and gross in nature
> Possess it merely.
>
>   (1.2.132–137)

When we interpreted this earlier, we were interested in the thematic context of 'corruption'. This clearly works with the generic context of revenge tragedy, where corruption is *the* main causal factor for the revenge. As such, the reading of the 'unweeded' extended metaphor and the focus on the historical ambiguity of semantic context of the word 'rank' (meaning both 'rotting' and 'vigorous') would stand. This would all be part of the more general 'Something is rotten in the state of Denmark' (1.4.90) theme. Indeed, with its play on the semantic context of 'state' (both *country* and *condition*), this statement becomes a touchstone for the revenge tragedy, where the corruption is social; in this case the court and the kingdom.

However, if we look at the same speech through the generic context of Greek tragedy, then our interpretation will change. In revenge tragedy the need for vengeance is obviously key. Vengeance is the necessary answer to an unjust state, where there is no legal means to bring power to book. Greek tragedy has a different way of contextualising events and thus giving them meaning. Let's focus for a moment on 'this world' at line 134. In our reading in Chapter 4, we noted a significant ambiguity. Does 'this world' refer to the corrupt court, or to the world more generally as it *seems* to Hamlet? That is, is this an objective reflection on the 'state of Denmark', or a subjective reflection on the 'state' of Hamlet? The Greek tragic context, with its stronger focus on the psychological suffering of the flawed hero – his *hamartia*, will concentrate our attention on the way Hamlet's inner darkness creates the atmosphere of corruption, bringing about his own tragic fall, or *peripeteia*. From this small detail, we can see how a shift in the generic context brings about a change in the way we frame key element of the play's language, and thus the way we understand its semantic, syntactic, thematic, and, as we shall see, iterative contexts. Of course, the beauty of close reading is that neither reading invalidates the other; they *enrich* each other. That said, reading *Hamlet* as a revenge tragedy will necessarily increase your focus on the social and political elements of the play, and, for example, Claudius and Polonius may become important characters. Reading it as a Greek tragedy, will mean a stronger engagement with Hamlet himself, especially his soliloquies, and his own inner tortures, perhaps making Gertrude and Ophelia more significant.

One way of consolidating this is to look at the most famous lines of the play, taking them as a **crux**, and see what effect the generic context can have on their meanings.

> To be, or not to be—that is the question;
> Whether 'tis nobler in the mind to suffer
> The slings and arrows of outrageous fortune,
> Or to take arms against a sea of troubles
> And by opposing end them;
>
> (3.1.55–59)

These lines begin with the most quoted iteration in English literature: 'To be, or not to be', where in the syntactic context, the word 'not' inverts the semantic context of 'to be'. Typically, this is taken to mean from *life* to *death*. However, it's rather odd, because there seems to be something of a non-sequitur as we widen the syntactic context of this first line. Lines 56–59 are to be about *revenge* rather than life and death. The semantic context of Hamlet's mixed metaphor presents a choice between *suffering* and *taking up arms*; that is, passively accepting, or actively revenging against 'a sea of troubles'. In the generic context of the revenge tragedy the 'sea of troubles' is Claudius' corrupt court. In this context, Hamlet's question of *being* or *not being* is not life, but rather the life of vengeance.

Of course, though, this is not the end of the soliloquy. There is a semi-colon, and the speech continues:

> to die; to sleep –
> No more, and by a sleep to say we end
> The heartache and the thousand natural shocks
> That flesh is heir to:
>
> (3.1.59–62)

Here Hamlet's focus is very much on 'not-being', and he draws on the conventional metaphor of death as '[n]o more' than 'a sleep': a comforting end to mortal sufferings. Though we can see this as part of the instability of the avenger, its depths come much more sharply into focus through the lens of Greek tragedy. Indeed, all thoughts of vengeance have gone, and we are again thematically concerned with the complexities of an interior life as they iterate across Hamlet's soliloquies. As the speech continues, Hamlet famously extends this metaphor, considering the afterlife as a dream that unsettles that sleep ('what dreams may come […] must give us pause' [65, 67]). We are back to Hamlet's tragic flaw, the way that his own anxious sufferings, contaminate even his metaphors, turning a consoling thought into troubling one. Through iteration, the flaw, *hamartia*, becomes *hubris*, a kind of self-indulgence that gives up on action in favour of melancholic thoughts.

Indeed, the soliloquy concludes as follows:

> Thus conscience does make cowards—
> And thus the native hue of resolution
> Is sicklied o'er with the pale cast of thought,
> And enterprises of great pitch and moment
> With this regard their currents turn awry,
> And lose the name of action.
>
> (3.1.82–87)

Here the two genres can be seen in direct conflict: the alliterated 'conscience' and 'cowards', exaggerated by the iterative rhythmic stresses on both the hard 'c's, emphasise *hamartia* and *hubris* at the expense of revenge. In our close reading, the semantic context of 'conscience' is worth dwelling on. In 1600, roughly the time of *Hamlet*'s creation, the *OED* tells us that *conscience* and *consciousness* were synonyms. It is not, then, as it would seem to a modern reader, *guilt* that makes Hamlet a coward, as much as *thought*, or self-knowledge. Guilt, of course, would be a consequence of revenge. Thought is what prevents it taking place. '[T]hinking too precisely on th'event' (4.4.40), as he will put it later. In the complex metaphor that follows line 83, the *hubris* of Hamlet's inner life is made plain in the complexion of his face: the tenor is the loss of the resolve to act; the vehicle is 'the native hue of resolution/Is sicklied o'er with the pale cast of thought'; the ground is the connection between thinking as stasis and illness as inactivity. Thinking, then, is opposed to action. This is a long way away from the initial question: 'To be or not to be'. The question itself is part of the problem – reflecting on the inner life is no way to revenge. It is Laertes, who learning of the murder of *his* father, rushes, sword drawn, into Claudius' court, who shows how revenge *should* be done. Laertes' act provides a useful iterative counterpart to the Greek tragedy of Hamlet's hubristic procrastination.

COMPLEXITY CASE STUDY

Perhaps the clearest indication that the generic context of Greek tragedy has become interpretively operative, even as a revenge tragedy should be taking place, is Hamlet's speech in Act 5. Not a soliloquy this time, but part of a conversation in prose with Horatio.

> *Hamlet:* We defy augury. There is special providence in the fall of a sparrow. If it be, 'tis not to come. If it be not to come, it will be now. If it be not now, yet it will come. The readiness is all, since no man of aught he leaves knows what it is to leave betimes. Let be.
>
> (5.2.197–202)

Here the iterative, thematic and generic contexts are all in play. The verb 'to be' – clearly a crux – is used in some form nine times in these lines. Iteratively and thematically, this picks up on the 'To be or not to be', but it is no longer about taking up arms against corruption; it is now about quietly 'suffer[ing] the slings and arrows of outrageous fortune'. If this is a revenge tragedy, then Hamlet has given up his role as avenger. Indeed, Claudius' death at the end of the play is not a planned revenge, but a spontaneous act, quite without forethought – *hubristic* or otherwise. Taking these lines in the generic context of Greek tragedy, however, we can see in them *anagnorisis* and *nemesis*. *Anagnorisis* is the recognition of truth. Here the 'truth' that Hamlet recognises is that even if our futures cannot be foreseen ('defy augury'), nevertheless they are fated ('special providence'). The anxiety about death in the earlier soliloquy is replaced with a calm acceptance: 'let be'. Letting fate take its course, then, ironically, to allow *nemesis* to enter the stage. It is Hamlet's acceptance of fate – of divine will, in the Greek tradition – that will lead to his own death, and to his revenge.

The bodies strewn over the stage at the end of Hamlet (Leartes, Gertrude, Claudius, and Hamlet himself), fit both Greek tragedy's conception of *catharsis*, in a pitiful resolution, and the *retributive violence* of the revenge tragedy. Fortinbras' assumption of the crown of Denmark, though, is a restoration of order that belongs more to the revenge tragedy. The Greek tragedy ends with Hamlet's death. The play has all the elements of both revenge and Greek tragedy in it; it is their competition that makes interpreting the play so fascinating, as the meaning of its many parts is wrested from one generic context to another.

4 THE NOVEL

Of all the major literary genres, the novel has the greatest possible range of generic contexts. The flexibility of the extended prose form has enabled an enormous diversity of styles and subjects: realism, historical novel, romance, fantasy, picaresque, science fiction, *bildungsroman*, eroticism, satire, the gothic, the comic, the postmodern, etc. It is almost by definition a 'mixed mode', and as such novels are very likely to be made up of more than one genre. The *fantasy* novel, for example, nearly always needs to draw on elements of *realism* in order to create something believable, such as the description of Bag End. But we will also need to have a different context in play to accept the presence of hobbits and dragons. Even so, when reading a novel, we are still likely to be guided by expectations and conventions, even if they are strained on occasion. As such, our close readings will be in part determined by generic contexts that cross over and, sometimes, even seem to contradict each other.

Wuthering Heights, which we looked at in an earlier chapter, is just such a novel. On the one hand we can see it as *realist*, and on the other as a *gothic*. Decisions about how to interpret the novel will depend on which generic context we use. Some very basic conventions of these two genres are set out in the following box (see Further Reading):

CONVENTIONS OF REALISM

a   Verisimilitude – e.g. presentation of life with richly detailed fidelity, giving the illusion of actual experience.

b   Set in a recognisable and locatable world.

c   Features the everyday, the normal, the pragmatic – childhood, adolescence, love, marriage, parenthood, infidelity, and death.

d   Ordinary middle- or working-class characters.

CONVENTIONS OF THE GOTHIC

a   Strong elements of the supernatural – e.g. ghosts, macabre and uncanny events.

b   Set in sprawling castles, with dark corridors, dungeons, secret passages; surrounded by wild, desolate landscapes.

c   Presiding atmosphere of gloom and terror.

d   Deals with aberrant psychological states.

e   Heroes and heroines in the direst of imaginable straits; wicked tyrants.

It might be that, as with *Hamlet*, you find one or other of these sets of conventions to be more appropriate. What I would like you consider, though, is the *effect* that choosing a different generic context will have on your reading of the novel's other contexts of close reading.

The novel certainly begins, as we have seen, with Lockwood's account of Heathcliff, as *realistic*. Indeed, Lockwood's description of Wuthering Heights' interior could almost be seen as a *locus classicus* of literary 'realism'. What follows is just a short extract:

> One stop brought us into the family sitting-room, without any introductory lobby or passage: they call it here 'the house' pre-eminently. It

includes kitchen and parlour, generally; but I believe at Wuthering Heights the kitchen is forced to retreat altogether into another quarter: at least I distinguished a chatter of tongues, and a clatter of culinary utensils, deep within; and I observed no signs of roasting, boiling, or baking, about the huge fireplace; nor any glitter of copper saucepans and tin cullenders on the walls. One end, indeed, reflected splendidly both light and heat from ranks of immense pewter dishes, interspersed with silver jugs and tankards, towering row after row, on a vast oak dresser, to the very roof. The latter had never been under-drawn: its entire anatomy lay bare to an inquiring eye, except where a frame of wood laden with oatcakes and clusters of legs of beef, mutton, and ham, concealed it.

(2)

This works to create **verisimilitude** in a few different ways. Most obviously, there is the syntactic context's piling up of details – the meticulously described space of the room, its furniture and objects. Each of these can, if necessary, be recognised as commonplace and conventional. As synecdoches they come together to create just what we'd expect in a large rural home of the period. Another important aspect of verisimilitude is the suggestion of a larger surrounding space – the noises heard from somewhere else in the house, the other kitchen 'deep within'; what's *not* in the room is as important to our sense of the room as what *is*. These further metonyms create a kind of multidimensional reality, where the space, the objects and Lockwood's interpretation of them represent something we can identify as *real*. This conforms to the first two conventions of realism cited above. Of course, not everything is described. That would be impossible. The semantic contexts of synecdoche and metonymy are used, as we've seen several times before, to create efficiency in the prose. Our imagination fills in the gaps as far as it needs to.

As we go on through the novel, we'll discover the other two conventions of realism: the presentation of everyday life, from childhood to death, and the novel's focus on middle- and working-class characters. Each of these conventions can be seen at work in Brontë's representation of Heathcliff. He very much reflects the focus on middle- and working-class characters. Indeed, the iterative context of the plot that we saw a couple of chapters ago traces Heathcliff's movement from servant to master. It also refuses to glamorise these iterations, rejecting the fairy tale or romance plot, in which Heathcliff would have had a noble lineage; likewise, the novel refuses to explain *how* he came by his income and gentlemanly manner. It is Isabella who, quite wrongly, sees Heathcliff as a 'hero of romance' (109). Ironically, perhaps, these iterated mysteries conform to the generic context of realism rather than stretching it too far, precisely because they don't let in anything too unusual. That said, we might well baulk at the idea that *all* the experiences presented to us in *Wuthering Heights* are exactly ordinary. There is, as suggested above, another, arguably conflicting, way to interpret key aspects of the novel's semantic, syntactic, iterative and thematic contexts.

Lockwood's 'dream', for example, seems to belong to a different generic context: the gothic. Forced by the weather to stay the night at Wuthering Heights, Lockwood is placed in bunk-come-closet in Heathcliff and Catherine's former bedroom. His sleep is disturbed by a branch knocking against the window.

> I remembered I was lying in the oak closet, and I heard distinctly the gusty wind, and the driving of the snow; I heard, also, the fir-bough repeat its teasing sound, and ascribed it to the right cause: but it annoyed me so much that I resolved to silence it, if possible; and, I thought, I rose and endeavoured to unhasp the casement. The hook was soldered into the staple: a circumstance observed by me when I was awake. I must stop it, nevertheless, I muttered, knocking my knuckles through the glass, and stretching an arm out to seize the importunate branch; instead of which, my fingers closed on the fingers of a little, ice-cold hand! The intense horror of nightmare came over me: I tried to draw back my arm, but the hand clung to it, and a most melancholy voice sobbed, 'Let me in – let me in!'

(17)

Here we seem to shift between *two* generic contexts. The passage begins in a realist frame, with detail and with credible connections between the events, but the moment Lockwood knocks his 'knuckles through the glass' we are in a different world. The domestic space of the house is suddenly intruded on by the gothic world of the moors. The creature, which a few lines later identifies itself as 'Catherine Linton', refuses to let go, and Lockwood cruelly rubs its small wrist on the broken glass of the window, 'till the blood ran down and soaked the bed clothes' (17). Still 'Catherine' won't let go. Our interpretation of this scene, and its place in the thematic context of the novel as a whole, depends entirely on which generic context we think we are in. *Realistically*, we can take each aspect of the dream and relate it back to a previous experience of Lockwood's. He had read about Catherine – as both Earnshaw and Linton (as she imagined her future husband) in the margins of an old bible he'd found in the closet. He learned there of her age, the date, her love for the moors, etc. The knocking is that of a pine branch against the window pane. As such, there is a 'reasonable' explanation for each semantic and syntactic element of the 'dream'. But the *gothic* generic context is also powerful. The 'ghost' of Catherine, the extreme terror, the unnecessary violence and the blood are all in excess of the constituent parts. If we take one word for analysis, 'nightmare', and locate it in its syntactic context ('the intense horror of *nightmare* came over me') we need to ask if it is *literal* or *figurative*? If its semantic context is literal, and this is a nightmare and no more, we are in a *realist* world. If it is figurative, and being used as a metaphor for Lockwood's feelings about something he feels to be really happening, then we are in a *gothic* world. Of course, we can't just take this scene in isolation. We'll only understand it when we've located in the wider context of the novel and as part of our re-reading cycle.

Heathcliff's immediate response is important. He clearly believes in the ghost, '[striking] his forehead with rage' (19) when Lockwood tells him that he had been visited by 'Catherine', 'the changeling' or 'wicked soul', who had been 'walking the earth these twenty years' (17, 18). We are clearly going to see the importance of this quite differently on a subsequent reading, when the full nature of Catherine and Heathcliff's relationship is available to us. Other characters, too, believe in aspects of the supernatural: Nelly believes in the portents of dreams (57); Catherine Earnshaw sees a ghost in her mirror (87–88); Joseph thinks he has seen Catherine and Heathcliff on the moors after Heathcliff's death (244–245), creating a context of credibility for the supernatural. But it is Heathcliff's actions that have the greatest thematic impact and the strongest effect on our re-reading. Towards the end of the novel, Heathcliff, who admits to 'a strong faith in ghosts' (209), tells Nelly that he once opened Catherine's grave, and stepping down into it, heard 'a sigh' at his ear: 'I knew no living thing in flesh and blood was by; but as certainly as you perceive the approach of some substantial body in the dark, though it cannot be discerned, so certainly I felt that Cathy was there' (210). At this point, as with 'nightmare' above, we need to make a choice. Is Heathcliff mad or self-deluded, and thus the novel's theme is a realist account of the psychological effects of grief; or should we believe in his experience, and allow the generic context of the gothic to guide our interpretation of the earlier scene, which despite being at the other end of the novel, is actually roughly contemporary to Heathcliff's admission? Of course, the novel is ambiguous. We cannot make that decision. Both generic contexts are at work and, as with *Hamlet*, it is the tension between them that makes the novel so remarkable.

The very last sentence of *Wuthering Heights* exemplifies this essential ambiguity. Lockwood, just prior to leaving the moors for good, visits the graves of Catherine, Edgar and Heathcliff: 'I lingered round them, under that benign sky: watched the moths fluttering among the heath and harebells; listened to the soft wind breathing through the grass; and wondered how anyone could ever imagine unquiet slumbers for the sleepers in that quiet earth' (245). The iterative tension between 'unquiet' and 'quiet' hangs on the difference between the realist and the gothic generic context. As such, they lead you back into and unsettled and ambivalent re-reading.

SUMMARY

As we become expert readers we internalise a huge range of generic conventions in relation to storytelling and poetic forms. These conventions provide us with expectations. These expectations, in turn, guide our interpretations. The function of a generic context in our close reading is to *limit* meaning; that is, to give a frame in which the complexities of the thematic, syntactic, semantic and iterative contexts are productively reduced. Remarkably, though, even relatively stable genres – like the sonnet or tragedy – still allow for a diverse and potentially conflicting range of close readings. Indeed, few genres are *pure*; such purity would quickly become tedious. Works very often grow more interesting, and more enjoyable, when they do something unexpected; that is, when another set of generic conventions come into the mix. Writers have, probably since the beginning of literary creation, used such mixing to enhance their creativity and, by teasing the reader, add to their pleasure.

FURTHER READING

M. H. Abrams. *A Glossary of Literary Terms*. 4th edn. New York: Holt, Rhinehart and Winston, 1981

J. A. Cuddon. *A Dictionary of Literary Terms*, Rev. C. E. Preston. London: Penguin, 1999.

Jonathan Culler. *Structuralist Poetics: Structuralism, Linguistics and the Study of Literature*. London: Routledge, 2002.

David Duff (ed.) *Modern Genre Theory*. London: Routledge, 2014

Helen Dubrow. *Genre*. London: Routledge, 2014.

David Lodge. *The Modes of Modern Writing: Metaphor, Metonymy, and the Typology of Modern Literature*. London: Bloomsbury, 2014.

Barbara Stanners. *Exploring Genre: Revenge Tragedy*. Putney: Phoenix, 2007.

THE ADVERSARIAL CONTEXT

We value literary texts because of what they do with language. The five contexts of close reading outlined in the foregoing chapters (semantic, syntactic, thematic, iterative and generic) are designed to focus your attention on that language so that you can get as much meaning and pleasure out of it as is possible. But what happens to our close readings if we are interested in things that are not so obviously *in* the texts that we are reading as those words on the page? For example, what if you wanted to explore whether Elizabeth Barrett Browning's life could be used to help you to close read her *Sonnets from the Portuguese*? Does it matter that she's a Victorian woman as well as a poet? How would it affect how we interpret the poems' words? Or in what ways might locating *The Great Gatsby* in the context of the American Dream enhance our close reading? Would that change of perspective also change the ways we understand and enjoy the novel? Or, what if we wanted to challenge the place of Heathcliff as the central character of *Wuthering Heights*, and instead focus our attention on its presenta-tion of female experience? How might that alter our appreciation of Brontë's novel?

These questions are very different to the kinds of questions we have been asking so far. What we would need to do in order to answer any of them is to reframe the text from a position *outside* the text, be it that of the life of the writer, or the historical moment of the text's produc-tion, or a theoretical position, like feminism. I am calling this reframing the **adversarial context**. Such contexts are adversarial, not because they are necessarily *against* the text, in the sense of taking contrary positions (though they often do), but because they begin with a *confrontation* between the text and some other kind of text – say, the texts of history or biography, the texts of Marxism or feminist discourse. That said, I wouldn't want you to think that the approach exemplified in the earlier chapters of this book doesn't also bring in questions from *outside* the text. Prosody, genre, the *OED* and even the aesthetic values that generate the judgments made in a close reading are all 'external' in some way. The explicit focus, however, of the first five contexts is the *words on the page*. The adversarial context is at least equally interested in a theory that is not, in essence, literary, and in ideas that aren't straightforwardly generated by the text itself.

There are many such adversarial approaches in addition to those already mentioned. Literary analysis employs ecocritical, psycho-analytic, new historical, structuralist, post-structuralist, deconstructive, post-colonialist, cognitive and queer theories, amongst others. These can all be used as adversarial contexts for a given literary text. The one thing, though, that *all* adversarial contexts need is *a foundation in the practice of close reading*. In this final chapter, I don't have the space to introduce you fully to the relationship between close reading and all the ideas and theories that makes up these adversarial contexts, but I shall present three short case studies that will demonstrate how close reading using the adversarial context can further your appreciation of literature.

CASE STUDY 1: BIOGRAPHY AND ELIZABETH BARRETT BROWNING'S *SONNETS FROM THE PORTUGUESE*

Elizabeth Barrett Browning's forty-four *Sonnets from the Portuguese* were written between 1844 and 1846, during her courtship with the poet Robert Browning. It was not until 1850, four years after they were married, that Elizabeth showed the poems to her husband. He encouraged their publication. The title *Sonnets from the Portuguese* was a deliberate deception, suggesting that the sequence was a translation of extant material rather than a poetic dramatisation of her own complex doubts, anxieties and feelings during her courtship. Such a deception was felt to be necessary, as a white middle-class Victorian woman's role was, ideally, domestic, supportive, spiritual, emotionally restrained and, above all, publicly *silent*. (Because of this, in the 1840s the Brontës were writing under male pseudonyms, as would George Eliot a generation later.) Even though Barrett Browning was already that rare thing, a published female poet, it was still felt prudent to supress the autobiographical nature of her poems' content as they dealt explicitly with her domestic life. Soon, however, it became widely known that the sonnet sequence represented *her* highly personal and impassioned experience and that the poems were autobiographical.

This, then, is a very brief biographical and historical context for Elizabeth Barrett Browning's *Sonnets from the Portuguese* (I refer you to the Further Reading for more detailed accounts). What we, as close readers, need to ask is 'in what ways can biography or history help us with our interpretation of the text's contexts of close reading?' Just as the qualities of sound in the iterative context only have traction when attached to the *language* of the text, history and biography are only significant for a *close reading* if they advance our interpretation of the work's semantic, syntactic, thematic, iterative or generic contexts. Let's see, then, what even this small amount of biographical and historical knowledge can do to enhance our reading of Sonnet XIII.

From the last chapter, you'll recall that the sonnet's first quatrain was about the inexpressibility of deep feeling, using the metaphor of a flickering torch held out between two faces, unable to clearly illuminate either of them. In the second quatrain, the speaker had another attempt at expressing the same idea. There she finds it equally impossible to hold out her 'spirit' for examination, as if it were a kind of proof of her feeling. Her emotions remained too deeply hidden. This failure of expression, then, became the **thematic context** of the poem. The sestet acknowledged this failure, but also uses the sonnet's *volta* to change the terms of what success might look like, making a case for the value of 'silence' for her 'womanhood'. I noted in that chapter that the connection between 'silence' and 'womanhood' might best be understood as part of larger Victorian cultural situation. The adversarial contexts of history and biography should be able to help us out.

To this end, let's look at the sonnet's sestet again:

> Nay, let the silence of my womanhood
> Commend my woman-love to thy belief,—
> And that I stand unwon, however wooed,
> And rend the garment of my life, in brief,
> By a most dauntless, voiceless fortitude,
> Lest one touch of this heart convey its grief.

To begin with I just want us to focus on that phrase in the sestet's first line 'the silence of my womanhood' and think how we can put specific biographical and historical sources to work in our close reading. In the case of Elizabeth Barrett Browning and Robert Browning, there is a most remarkable and useful resource: their letters. During the two years of their courtship, the very period in which Elizabeth was writing the sonnets, they sent hundreds of letters to each other, which are all available online in a text searchable form (see Further Reading). As with the *OED*, we can search for the word 'silence' and see in what settings it can be found. We can then use our thematic context of failure of expression to select appropriate meanings, enriching our readings.

Extracts from three early letters from Elizabeth to Robert, chosen in just this way, read as follows. In each case we are interested in the context of the word 'silence'.

If you did but know dear Mr Browning how often I have written .. not this letter I am about to write, but another better letter to you, .. in the midst of my *silence*, .. you w[oul]d not think for a moment that the east wind, with all the harm it does to me, is able to do the great harm of putting out the light of the thought of you to my mind – for this, indeed, it has no power to do. I had the pen in my hand once to write – & why it fell out, I cannot tell you.

(17th April, 1845; emphasis added)

Which reminds me to observe that you are so restricting our vocabulary, as to be ominous of *silence* in a full sense, presently. First, one word is not to be spoken – and then, another is not. And why?

(21st May, 1845; emphasis added)

I intended to write to you last night & this morning, & could not – you do not know what pain you give me in speaking so wildly – And if I disobey you my dear friend, in speaking, (I for my part) of your wild speaking, I do it, not to displease you, but to be in my own eyes & before God, a little more worthy, or less unworthy, of a generosity from which I recoil by instinct & at the first glance, yet conclusively – & because my *silence* w[oul]d be the most disloyal of all means of expression, in reference to it.

(23rd May, 1845; emphasis added)

The first extract is, almost, a prose version of the sonnet itself. It recounts Elizabeth's failed attempts to communicate something better to Robert, as well as containing references to a harmful wind, and of putting out a light, and a failure to write. The 'silence' seems to be an imagined letter that ought to be written, but can't be because of the limits of expression. The second extract blames Robert for a restriction on vocabulary, and thus Elizabeth's silence is enforced 'in a full sense' – there are no more words. In the third extract, it is Robert whom she must disobey in order to speak about what it is that has upset her – his 'wild words'. Silence, though, would be more disloyal, so she does, in the end, write the letter; its convoluted syntax mirroring her anxieties. In each case 'silence' and difficulty of expression are explicitly connected, but the syntactic contexts give 'silence' a slightly different semantic context. First, it is her own failure, second it is Robert's restrictions, and third it is Robert's 'wild' words. Though I think there are a range of connections to the sonnet as a whole that you may already be thinking of, here I want to restrict the use of these letters to that word 'silence'. But first I would also like to bring out the biographical and historical semantic context of 'womanhood'.

In the case of 'womanhood' the letters are less helpful. There is only one use of the word in her letters to Robert: 'the work of my earliest youth, half childhood half *womanhood*, was published in 1826' (15–17th July, 1845; emphasis added). Womanhood, here, is a phase of maturity. In this case a more useful historical source is the *OED*, especially if we put the definition of womanhood next to contemporary mid-nineteenth century usages:

- Women considered collectively; womankind. 1858: 'The infinite wrongs, errors, and sufferings of this mass of womanhood.'
- The state, condition, or fact of being a woman rather than a man. Tennyson, 1859: 'She, with all grace Of womanhood and queenhood, answer'd him.'
- The disposition, character, or qualities traditionally attributed to women; womanliness. Dickens in 1841: 'Miss Brass's maiden modesty and gentle womanhood.'

We can discern a tension here in the mid-century semantic context of 'womanhood' between the acknowledgement of women's wrongs and sufferings and the Victorian ideals of grace, queenhood, modesty, gentleness. Barrett Browning's 'silence' in the sonnet could be aligned to either of these aspects of woman-hood's semantic context: she is silent as wronged (silenc*ed*), or she is silent as befits her grace and modesty. Either way her silence is metonymic for a particular historical sense of 'womanhood' that her letters and her poems are exploring.

If we take 'silence' to be attached to the wrongs of 'womanhood', then we can see Robert as a silenc*er*. The second and third letter extracts certainly support that. If we take 'silence' to be attached to the Victorian ideas of 'womanhood', then we are closer to the sense of silence in the first extract; it is self-imposed. Either way we get an enhanced sense of the possibilities of those two terms in their syntactic context. This interpretation is further modified when we relocate the words in the wider syntactic context of the sestet. Here we get the sense that silence is the braver choice ('dauntless') and the more determined choice ('fortitude'). Her voicelessness is not a lack of power, or something imposed by Robert, it is rather Barrett Browning's *refusal* to use a power that could damage her love, the expression of which could lead to its opposite: 'grief'. From this we can see that locating the word 'silence' **adversarially**, as a crux of the semantic, syntactic and generic contexts offers us a more complex and subtle close reading of the sonnet.

In many ways, this reading may be more satisfying, as if we are now getting to Elizabeth Barrett Browning's *intentions*, rather than just coming up with our own interpretation.

We do, though, need to be cautious with biography. First, we are reliant on the biographical and historical sources we have researched, such as the letters. The letters themselves, as literary artefacts, are highly complex and could certainly be interpreted in different ways. Second, not all authors have reliable or available biographies – Shakespeare is the most obvious example, so a reliance on his biography could leave us little to say. Third, bio-graphical and historical readings are often reductive: as though biography or influence can explain creativity, or conjure away ambiguity. Finally, and this was certainly the case with Barrett Browning's sonnets, an overtly biographical interpretation can make works seem unsatisfactory: too limited to a single experience, too personal, too much out of the mainstream to be interesting. Indeed, until they were recovered by feminist critics in the early 1980s, Barrett Browning's sonnets had been ignored critically for a century *precisely because* of their association with what was long seen as a very specific and all too familiar sentimental epistolary Victorian romance, a genre too closely associated with women writers and their domestic concerns to be taken seriously. So, even though biography and history, if available, will nearly always bring interesting evidence to bear on our interpretation, shaping the contexts of close reading from the semantic to the thematic and generic, they are *not* the keys to unlock a literary riddle. They are, rather, additional contexts which at their best augment a text's enjoyable complexity.

FURTHER READING

Roland Barthes. 'The Death of the Author' and 'From Work to Text'. *Image/Music/Text*. Trans. Stephen Heath. London: Fontana, 1977, 142–148, 155–164.

The Browning Letters. Baylor. http://digitalcollections.baylor.edu/cdm/portal/collection/ab-letters. Accessed 15/9/17.

Dorothy Mermin. [1981] 'The Female Poet and the Embarrassed Reader: Elizabeth Barrett Browning's Sonnets from the Portuguese', in Harold Bloom, ed., *Elizabeth Barrett Browning*. Philadelphia: Chelsea House, 2002.

Dorothy Mermin. *Elizabeth Barrett Browning: The Origins of a New Poetry*. Chicago: University of Chicago Press, 1989.

Mary Sanders Pollock. Elizabeth Barrett and Robert Browning: A Creative Partnership. London: Ashgate, 2003.

Rebecca Stott. 'Genre: A Chapter on Form', in Simon Avery and Rebecca Stott, *Elizabeth Barret Browning*. Edinburgh: Pearson, 2003.

Marianne Van Remoortel. '(Re)gendering Petrarch: Elizabeth Barrett Browning's Sonnets from the Portuguese'. *Tulsa Studies in Women's Literature* 25(2) (2006): 247–266.

W. K. Wimsatt. 'The Intentional Fallacy'. *The Verbal Icon: Studies in the Meaning of Poetry*. London: Methuen, 1970.

CASE STUDY 2: MARXISM AND *THE GREAT GATSBY*

In this second case study I shall use the example of Marxist literary theory, which is, fundamentally, interested in two things: first, the economic aspects of a text; second, the relationship between the classes. A basic insight of Marxism is that the economic inequality of a class structure is maintained by cultural forms like literature because these forms will often naturalise that economic hierarchy, preventing people from recognising that they are exploited. Hareton Earnshaw's regaining of his family's house and land at the close of *Wuthering Heights* is a case in point: in the plot, his wealth is a *natural* inheritance which seems like justice. Marxists call this process, whereby culture reproduces class structures in the interest of the ruling class, 'ideology.' What Marxist critics look for is the ways in which literary texts present ideology in order to demonstrate how it replicates a specific hierarchy, or, where possible, to discover tensions within that ideology that would expose it as false. The rise of Heathcliff and the inversion of 'master' and 'servant' is an example of such a tension *within* ideology; though, of course, it is resolved by Hareton's inheritance. Marxist critics are very aware that texts often both challenge *and* reinforce the dominant ideology of their time. *The Great Gatsby* is a text which can be shown, through close reading, to do both these things.

In the broadest sense, the ideology in place in the period in which *The Great Gatsby* is set and written – the United States in the 1920s – is capitalism. There is, though, a more culturally specific version of capitalist ideology in place in *Gatsby*, namely 'the American Dream'; a term coined in 1917 by David Graham Lennox. The American Dream has a very specific ideological function: to give every American the belief that they can 'make it'; that is, that they can become rich. Ideologically this functions by creating a culture of aspiration where the 'dream' of wealth can be sustained even amidst 'real' conditions of poverty and exploitation. In this way, for Marxist critics, ideology becomes an engine through which a few may 'succeed' and fuel the dream, but because of which most will struggle on with only their hopes intact. They are exploited by the capitalist machine while *dreaming* of something better.

In order to enhance our close reading by using an adversarial context we simply take the preoccupations of the theory in question and use them as a thematic context. In this case we'll take Marxist issues, specifically the ideological veiling of static class and economic relationships by the American Dream, and use these to select appropriate passages for our close reading. In the novel Jay Gatsby is typically taken to be an embodiment of the American Dream. He has raised himself from nothing to a position of wealth and status. He is a success. How does the veil of ideology work here? It works by hiding economic value behind those of a romance. As such, material achievement is, for Gatsby, beside the point. He's *not* in it for the money; what Gatsby *thinks* he wants is Daisy.

As Nick's narrative presents her, Daisy's attractions seem to belong to one characteristic: her voice. It is here that we get into the language of the text, and can put to work some of our familiar tools – especially the semantic, iterative and thematic contexts. When Nick first encounters Daisy he describes her 'low, thrilling voice. It is the kind of voice that the ear follows up and down, as if each speech is an arrangement of notes that will never be played again' (14). The ground of the simile compares Daisy's voice to a musical improvisation. But it is the *sound* that matters, not what she says. Her actual words are mundane, even banal: 'Do they miss me?', 'How gorgeous! Let's go back, Tom. Tomorrow!' (14). A few pages later, Nick describes how Daisy's voice 'compelled me forward breathlessly' (18). For Nick it is 'as if her heart was trying to come out to you concealed in one of those breathless, thrilling words' (18). Again, Daisy is 'extemporizing' and her actual words are bland enough: 'You remind me of a – a rose, an absolute rose. Doesn't he?' (18). Daisy's voice – its *sound*, rather than the words she says – is established, through the iterative and semantic contexts, as a metonym of desire. Daisy seems to effortlessly charm Nick through the timbre and rhythms of her speech. Even Jordon corroborates Nick's feelings, recognising 'something in that voice of hers' (71). Daisy, then, like Keats' nightingale, is established by the narrative as *naturally* attractive and, as such, a worthwhile object of desire in her own right. Anything that appears to be natural is, from the adversarial context of Marxism, highly suspicious. For Marxists, remember, ideology is the naturalisation of exploitative economic hierarchies.

In an adversarial context, then, Nick's narration makes sense of Gatsby's attraction to Daisy. Gatsby's pursuit of money is not a pursuit of money in and of itself, it is a pursuit of Daisy, whose semantic context, constructed through iteration, is desirability itself. This, then, is *romantic* love, not grubby economics, and certainly not ideology (we can compare this to Heathcliff's mysterious financial self-improvement, with its end of winning Catherine from Edgar). The novel, though, doesn't let this reading stand. Surprisingly it's Gatsby himself who sees through the veil. Gatsby and Nick have visited Tom and Daisy's house, and they are all getting ready to leave for the city, Nick and Gatsby are standing in their driveway, waiting:

> Gatsby turned to me rigidly:
> 'I can't say anything in this house, old sport.'
> 'She's got an indiscreet voice,' I remarked. 'It's full of – ' I hesitated.
> 'Her voice is full of money,' he said suddenly.
> That was it. I'd never understood before. It was full of money – that was the inexhaustible charm that rose and fell in it, the jingle of it, the cymbals' song of it ... High in a white palace the king's daughter, the golden girl ...
>
> (106)

Daisy's all but impossible voice, with its thrilling low throb, its improvisatory charm, is transformed by Gatsby's key thematic revelation. The adversarial context of ideology will interpret this as a stark admission of the *economic* basis of Daisy's attraction. Gatsby's 'love' is not a higher romance, it is wholly in line with material aspirations of the American Dream. Nick's interpretation of Gatsby's insight is also of ideological value, as he clearly misses (or ignores) any political ramifications. For Nick it *explains* her musicality, but her 'charm' remains 'inexhaustible'. Nick sees no contradiction between the material and the romantic. Indeed, to reinforce this, he immediately reaches for the generic context of the romance, and places Daisy 'High in a white palace the king's daughter', and thus re-naturalises Gatsby's attraction to her. But, for the Marxist, the cat is out of the bag. Daisy is *not* a metonym for desire in general, but, as an adversarial close reading reveals, she is a metonym for wealth. That is why what she says never matters. It is what her attainment represents for Gatsby that's important, and that is 'money'.

In case we missed it, the novel makes it clear once again in the next chapter. Nick is relating the story of Gatsby's pre-war relationship with Daisy, when as a young officer, Gatsby had been invited back to Daisy's house:

> Her porch was bright with the bought luxury of star-shine; the wicker of the settee squeaked fashionably as she turned toward him and he kissed her curious and lovely mouth. She had caught a cold, and it made her voice huskier and more charming than ever, and Gatsby was overwhelmingly aware of the youth and mystery that wealth imprisons and preserves, of the freshness of many clothes, and of Daisy, gleaming like silver, sage and proud above the hot struggles of the poor.
>
> (132)

What our adversarial appreciation of this passage should pick out is the way that romance, again, is syntactically contextualised in economic terms: the 'bought luxury of star-shine'; the preservation of 'youth and mystery' by 'wealth'; Daisy's 'many clothes'; Daisy 'gleaming like silver ... above the hot struggles of the poor'. The thematic, syntactic and semantic contexts that we have been outlining all come together in the iterated crux of Daisy's voice. It is not the huskiness of the cold that gives it its attractiveness – that is Nick's defence against the ideological truth – it is the material conditions of the encounter.

What we learn from our Marxist adversarial close reading is that there is an important difference between Nick as *narrator* and Fitzgerald as *author*. Nick, half in love with Daisy and Gatsby himself, seems to hide from the truth the author presents even though he is revealing it in his narration. This is powerfully, and pleasurably, ironic; it gives a rich layering to our reading. Nick is a believer in the American Dream, hence his bitter disappointment at Gatsby's failure, which he veils from himself by turning the story into a romance. Fitzgerald, it could be argued, has seen through that same American Dream, even while his characters retain what Marxists call their 'false consciousness'. As such, the novel challenges *and* preserves the ideology that structures its thematic context and these tensions are revealed through each of the contexts of close reading, semantic, syntactic, iterative and generic, if we frame them using the adversarial context of Marxism.

FURTHER READING

Louis Althusser. 'Ideology and Ideological State Apparatuses.' *Lenin and Philosophy and Other Essays*. London: New Left Books, 1971, 135–149.

Peter Barry. 'Marxist Criticism.' *Beginning Theory*. Manchester: Manchester University Press, 2002, 156–171.

Catherine Belsey. *Critical Practice*. 2nd edn. London: Routledge, 2002.

Terry Eagleton, ed. *Ideology*. London: Routledge, 2013.

Raymond Williams. *Marxism and Literature*. Oxford: Oxford University Press, 1977.

CASE STUDY 3: FEMINISM AND *WUTHERING HEIGHTS*

In the analysis of *Wuthering Heights* using the iterative and generic contexts that I offered in Chapters 5 and 7 my focus was on Heathcliff. He was the protagonist whose unexpected arrival starts the 'plot' and whose death completes its iterations. He was used as my example of a character's 'credible continuity'. His interpretation of events was even offered as the most significant validation of a gothic reading of the novel's generic context. I hope you saw this as a fair and reasonable reading of the novel. But maybe you didn't; maybe you thought I was missing too much out or ignoring key aspects of the book. Indeed, there are very good reasons to question my choices about what matters in the novel. Why should *Heathcliff's* iterations make up the plot? Why should *his* character be taken as representative? Why should *his* opinion by used as a validation of the generic context? A feminist critic, taking an adversarial position, might well ask why I have valued *Heathcliff's* overtly masculine rise to power over the experiences of the principal female characters in the novel: Nelly, and the two Catherines; or why I have not considered the importance of Heathcliff's masculinity in my analysis. These are valid questions. Feminist literary scholars act to refocus critical practice to ensure that the representation of *female* experience is fully accounted for, to ensure that texts by women writers are appropriately appreciated, and to ensure that gender – both masculine and feminine – is explored.

Such an **adversarial context** will, of course, make a crucial difference to how the contexts of close reading are deployed, and, as with the Marxists in the previous example, the preoccupations of feminist critics will become **thematic contexts** for our analysis.

In this final case study, we shall use the adversarial context of feminism to revisit the **generic context** of the gothic. You'll recall that a summary of its conventions looked like this:

a   Strong elements of the supernatural – e.g. ghosts, macabre and uncanny events.

b   Set in sprawling castles, with dark corridors, dungeons, secret passages; surrounded by wild, desolate landscapes.

c   Presiding atmosphere of gloom and terror.

d   Deals with aberrant psychological states.

e   Heroes and heroines in the direst of imaginable straits; wicked tyrants.

In the analysis in Chapter 7, I focused on the first of these conventions, contrasting the realistic and the supernatural. The other four conventions are equally applicable, but we do have to do a bit more work with convention (b) 'set in sprawling castles, with dark corridors, etc.' Now, there is often something interesting going on where a convention doesn't quite fit, and as such these are good places to focus a close reading. I'm going to explore this lack of fit in this case study.

The medieval castle, as re-imagined by the gothic, is a masculine space: the domain of the 'wicked tyrant' and a place of danger and imprisonment for the female heroine. Wuthering Heights is certainly an *old* building, and it has 'a quantity of grotesque carving lavished over the front' (2); but from our introduction to its kitchen we recognise it as a *domestic* space, rather than a typical gothic castle. Thrushcross Grange is an even more ordered family home, and certainly a domestic rather than a gothic space. Domestic space in the nineteenth century was culturally held to be feminine. For the Victorian woman the home was a refuge where she was protected from the masculine harshness of the outside world and could express herself through the governance of her household. The home as a refuge sharply contrasts with the gothic convention of the castle. What we have done here is to reframe the generic within the adversarial context, which guides us to ask questions about gender, namely, 'how and why is a normatively feminine domestic space functioning as the masculine space of a gothic castle?' This, in turn, becomes the guiding theme for our adversarial appreciation of *Wuthering Heights*.

When analysing a longer text like a novel, it is important to consider relationships between part and whole, and thus to find evidence from across the novel's breadth. As we are concerned with gendered domestic and gothic spaces, it would be sensible to look for iterations that form cruxes between the domestic and the gothic in the novel's two houses, Wuthering Heights and Thrushcross Grange. One such passage occurs towards the beginning of Nelly's narrative, when she tells Lockwood about Heathcliff and Catherine's spying through the window of the Grange during a late evening ramble across the moor. The scene they see through the glass is almost ideally domestic: a well-furnished, brightly lit house, inhabited by two impeccably dressed children, Edgar and Isabella Linton. As Heathcliff puts it 'ah! – it was beautiful – a splendid place carpeted with crimson, and crimson covered chairs and tables, and a pure white ceiling bordered by gold' (33). Heathcliff thinks the place 'heaven', but Edgar and Isabella are bitterly arguing over a tiny lapdog, and with a gothic sensibility, Heathcliff observes that Isabella 'lay screaming at the farther end of the room, shrieking as if witches were running red-hot needs into her' (33). Laughing at their stupidity, Catherine and Heathcliff are overheard, and the Linton's bull-dog is let loose. It grabs Catherine by the ankle, and she is caught and injured. The Lintons take her into the Grange and, recognising her, feed her cakes and comb her hair. Symbolically, she passes into the Linton's domestic 'heaven' and away from the hell of the Heights. Five weeks later, healed from the dog bite, she returns to the Heights transformed by her stay. As Nelly puts it, rather than a 'wild, hatless little savage', she is now 'a very dignified person' (36). From this point on there is a divide in Catherine, a divide that exactly matches our gendered gothic binarism. This divide is between the girl who loves the moors, thematically tied to her love for Heathcliff, and the Heights, and a young lady with aspirations for the domestic beauties of Thrushcross Grange, thematically tied to Edgar Linton. We know, of course, that during Heathcliff's long absence, Catherine marries Edgar and, with that, chooses the domesticity of the Grange. This does not, however, resolve the thematic tensions within her.

These tensions reawaken when Heathcliff returns. At first he meets Catherine regularly at the Grange, with Edgar's grudging acceptance. But, after a violent quarrel, Edgar refuses to let Catherine see Heathcliff again. Catherine locks herself in her bedroom and refuses to eat. On being misled by Nelly that Edgar is unconcerned by her absence, Catherine becomes deranged. She tears her pillow with her teeth and demands that Nelly open the window in her bedroom. After Nelly refuses, Catherine's behaviour becomes increasingly strange. She categorises the feathers from her torn pillow by bird species, reminding us of her close relationship with the wild moors. Then she becomes convinced that her reflection in her mirror is a ghost. Increasingly agitated, Catherine then imagines she is 'lying in [her] chamber at Wuthering Heights', hearing the firs in the wind outside her lattice-window. From what Catherine says to Nelly, it appears that during her illness she has been suffering a delusion that she actually was 'enclosed in the oak-panelled bed at home' her 'heart ach[ing] with some great grief' (91). In her vision, Catherine forgets her married life and all her time since, as a child, she first came to Thrushcross Grange. As she puts it to Nelly:

> But, supposing at twelve years old, I had been wrenched from the Heights, and every early association, and my all in all, as Heathcliff was at that time, and been converted at a stroke into Mrs Linton, the lady of Thrushcross Grange, and the wife of a stranger: an exile, and an outcast, thenceforth, from what had been my world – you may fancy a glimpse of the abyss where I grovelled!
>
> (91)

This moment from her past, the separation from Heathcliff that began when they looked through the window together, is recognised as *the* moment of crisis. She rejects her gradual acculturation to married domestic life; rejects that she *chose* to become 'Mrs Linton, the lady of Thrushcross Grange', and imagines this change had happened 'at a stroke'. The consequence is that she feels she is an 'exile' from the *outside*, from her true home, the moors and the Heights. The Grange's people are strangers to her deepest nature and her life at the Grange is an imprisonment which she has forced upon her*self*. In this state of self-incarceration her bedroom has become an 'abyss'; that is, a masculine gothic space. She once more demands that Nelly 'Open the window again wide: fasten it open!' (91). When Nelly refuses, she says 'You won't give me the chance of life' (91). Catherine opens it herself 'and ben[ds] out, careless of the frosty air that cut[s] about her shoulders keen as a knife' (91). Though the Heights are invisible from the Grange, in her delusion Catherine claims to see its lit windows in the dark night. These imagined pinpoints of light are her way back into to its space; a space that represents her free childhood.

Catherine's delusions directly recall Lockwood's supernatural dream and the refuge that the Heights is for the little ghost 'Catherine *Linton*'. As she put it, 'I'm come home: I'd lost my way on the moor!' (17). For the ghost the Heights is also refuge. Why, then, is the ghost called Linton, rather than Earnshaw? As Lockwood asks, 'why did I think of *Linton*? I had read *Earnshaw* twenty times for Linton' (18). Lockwood's choice of names, of course, is only possible because of Catherine's fantasies about her own future – she had been testing out the names of her possible husbands in the writings that prompt Lockwood's dream. The change of name indicates a change of identity; but it is a change that brings about a loss. For Catherine *Linton*, Thrushcross Grange is a haunted gothic prison, and Edgar, to her mind, is her gaoler. For Catherine, in an inversion of the Victorian feminine ideal, the *domestic* is the prison and the *gothic* wilderness of the moors and the violent space of the Heights are her refuge. In each case the gothic elements of the generic context, when considered in the adversarial context of feminism, are inverted and through this inversion they become symbolic of *gendered* anxieties about marriage and the domestic sphere; about a woman's role in the nineteenth century, where the one thing, the novel suggests, that she can't do, is choose to be herself. She must choose to identify with a man and in so doing become 'domestic'; a domesticity which is figured as a gothic gaol. When we read this adversarially, the personal and private concerns of Catherine Earnshaw become a way of understanding the political concerns of an epoch.

We can pursue this further by considering what happens to the generic context at the end of the novel. At first the Heights becomes conventionally gothic when Heathcliff kidnaps Catherine and Edgar's daughter, who you'll recall is also called Catherine, in order to force her to marry his son (a key part of the inheritance plot). Interestingly, and satisfyingly, the younger Catherine uses her mother's closet-bedroom window to escape: 'she got easily out of its lattice, and on to the ground, by means of the fir tree, close by' (207). The 'ghost' Catherine Linton's escape *into* the *refuge* of the Heights becomes the 'real' Catherine Linton's mode of escape *from* the Heights as a gothic *prison*. This iterative use of Catherine's window, the very place where Lockwood had his dream, seems to perfectly capture the ambivalence at the heart of the novel, where Wuthering Heights is both refuge and prison, domestic and gothic. This ambivalence is, at least in part, resolved in the final scenes of the novel.

On Lockwood's last visit to the Heights, now with a flower garden and open doors and windows, he spies the younger Catherine 'not far from one of the windows' (223). She is stood just behind Hareton and teaching him to read. In sharp contrast to the earlier scene with Edgar and Isabella, this scene presents unambiguous domestic contentment, as an embarrassed Lockwood quickly realises. Hareton's wildness, the influence of Heathcliff, is being repaired by Catherine's teaching, teaching that she received from her father, Edgar. Though there was no contentment in *Wuthering Heights* for the first Catherine, or for Heathcliff, whose gothic characters don't fit in the nineteenth century, there is for their counterparts of the next generation. Hareton comes into the property, as we noted in the last chapter, but it is the younger Catherine's domesticating influence that creates the conditions for their contentment. Hareton's threatening masculinity is 'softened' (223) and Catherine's femininity is given a space in which she can reign as Hareton's wife, and thus, ironically, as Catherine *Earnshaw*. The home, with its now wide-open windows, is for both a refuge rather than a prison. Domesticity, rather than the gothic, *seems* to prevail in this adversarial analysis. But, in our close reading of the whole, we need to attend to those last words of the novel, as we did above. The original Catherine Earnshaw and Heathcliff still have a haunting gothic presence if we *do* 'imagine unquiet slumbers for the sleepers in that quiet earth' (245). As such, we might conclude, adversarially, that the female spirit of Catherine, with its gothic wildness, has not been wholly subsumed by the Victorian ideals of womanhood.

FURTHER READING

Peter Barry. 'Feminist Criticism'. *Beginning Theory*. 3rd edn. Manchester: Manchester University Press, 2009, 121–138.

Sandra M. Gilbert and Susan Gubar. *The Madwoman in the Attic: The Woman Writer and the Nineteenth-Century Literary Imagination*. New Haven CT: Yale University Press, 1984.

J. Hillis Miller. 'Wuthering Heights: Repetition and the Uncanny'. *Fiction and Repetition: Seven English Novels*. Cambridge MA: Harvard University Press, 1982.

Toril Moi. *Sexual/Textual Politics*. 2nd edn. London: Routledge, 2002.

Lyn Pykett. 'Gender and Genre in Wuthering Heights'. *Wuthering Heights: Contemporary Critical Essays*. Ed. Patsy Stoneman. London: Palgrave, 1993, 86–99.

CONCLUSION
ADVERSARIAL APPRECIATION AND THE FUTURES OF CLOSE READING

At the outset of this guide I asked three questions: What happens when we read? Why do we enjoy reading? How can we understand reading, and by understanding it enjoy it even more? I think we can now offer some answers to those questions. First, what happens when we read is, perhaps, not what we might have intuitively thought happened. We've learned that meaning does not exist within individual words and, as such, it is not just built up from an aggregate of those individual words. Rather, meaning exists in the relationships *between* words: the ways in which they work together. Reading is grasping those relationships. The contexts of close reading, as I've set them out above, are one way of drawing attention to these relationships and creating an appropriate method for their analysis. Does knowing this help us to understand *why* we enjoy reading? What it tells us is that reading is not just passively following lines of words with the eye, it's actually an act of creation. The meanings that are evoked by the relationships between words don't happen on the page, they happen in our heads. That, I think, is why we enjoy reading. It is because we are active and involved in the creation of what we read when we read. Does knowing this, and having a method to understand it and express it, help us to enjoy reading even more? If so, that would answer the final question. Of course, the real answer to this question is up to you. Now that you have a new way of grasping what goes on in literary works and a methodology that you can apply to release their complexity, will you enjoy reading more than you did before? I can only answer: I hope so. I hope that your attitude to literature, your confidence with it, and your enjoyment of it have all been enhanced.

A good word for this increased reading pleasure is 'appreciation'. Fittingly, the semantic context of 'appreciation' (so our familiar friend the *OED* tells me) has a range of meanings that each offer something in this context. There is 'appreciation' as an 'increase in value' (the price of Shakespeare's *Folio* has *appreciated*); there is 'appreciation' as gratitude (I *appreciate* all that Shakespeare has done for English drama); there is 'appreciation' as a recognition of the value of excellence (I *appreciate* Shakespeare's insight into human nature); finally (and perhaps this is the first one you thought of) there is 'appreciation' as 'understanding subtleties and complexities' (I can now better *appreciate* the profundity of Shakespeare's tragic vision). All four of these meanings are appropriate for the kind of appreciation of literary language advanced here: increase in value, gratitude, excellence, and understanding complexity. Appreciation in each of these senses, and even more so cumulatively, evokes the kind of satisfaction that, in the first chapter, I called *analytic pleasure*.

Nevertheless, appreciation alone is not a sufficient response to a literary text. Despite any enhanced appreciation the contexts of close reading may provide, texts should not be enjoyed merely as isolated works of genius, cut off from the world that created them and that continues to consume them. Hence the expression at the head of this conclusion: *adversarial* appreciation. We will often need to challenge what we appreciate – hold it to account for its ideological shortcomings, understand its historical limitations, critique its inner tensions and explore its silences and ruptures. In so doing we will learn something valuable about both the world from which the text emerged and the cultures which are now 'appreciating' it. In the last chapter we began to see this at work as we looked at the adversarial context. As the outermost context, the adversarial context will often make significant changes to the meanings of the five inner contexts. Indeed, though a text may remain relatively stable, theories will always be shifting as they aim to answer the questions raised by our ever-changing contemporary concerns. What *matters* for a close reading, then, will always be reshaped. Even so, the methodology for the practice of close reading that you've learned across the foregoing chapters should be both robust and flexible enough to withstand the shifting adversarial environment. Let's take a very quick look at some examples of current and emergent literary critical positions and see in what ways they change our interpretations of by now familiar texts, while working with the contexts of close reading.

Ecocriticism is a literary theory that has come to prominence over the last decade (though its origins are much earlier – see Further Reading), and its rise is no doubt a timely response to wider ecological concerns. Its fundamental principle is to consider literary environments – typically the settings of texts – to be as important as the more established and familiar adversarial contexts of class, race and gender, and as such worthy of study in their own right. What this often amounts to is an inversion in which the background or setting becomes the foreground, and the typical foreground (e.g. character and plot) becomes the background. As such, the adversarial context of ecocriticism reframes our close reading and changes the way we attend to the semantic, syntactic, thematic, iterative and generic contexts. To explain this we can briefly return to a passage we looked at in the very first chapter of this book:

> In a hole in the ground there lived a hobbit. Not a nasty, dirty, wet hole, filled with the ends of worms and an oozy smell, nor yet a dry, bare, sandy hole with nothing in it to sit down on or to eat: it was a hobbit-hole, and that means comfort.

(11)

When I read this passage above, my interest was in pointing out the strange familiarity of the setting and in explaining how it would become metonymic for the semantic context of the word 'hobbit'. As such, in that earlier reading a hobbit was seen as belonging to a world that negates the discomforts of nature – nasty, dirty, wet, oozy, etc., and is therefore comfortable and civilised. An ecocritical close reading would invert this, and focus its attention on what is *negated* here and why and ask: 'what attitude to the natural world is being evoked?' This would then become a thematic context, and we would look at other passages and consider how nature is being represented; as, for example, in this passage that I also looked at in the first chapter:

> Now they had gone far on into the Lone-Lands, where there were no
> people left, no inns, and the roads grew steadily worse. Not far ahead
> were dreary hills, rising higher and higher, dark with trees. On some
> of them were old castles with an evil look, as if they had been built by
> wicked people. Everything seemed gloomy, for the weather that day
> had taken a nasty turn.
>
> (47)

In the reading of this in the first chapter, I was concerned with
issues of time, space, world-creation and Bilbo's feelings. From an
ecocritical perspective, where the adversarial guides the thematic,
this interpretation would change. What matters for our close
reading now is *why* the wilderness is depicted as so threatening
and unremittingly gloomy. *Why* is the natural landscape associated thematically with evil? The semantic and thematic contexts
of each word we look at have become differently charged, and an
ecocritically themed close reading of *The Hobbit* would want to
explore why it is that 'wilderness' in the novel is consistently
associated with danger, while comfort is associated with a kind of
agrarian ideal of settled, farmed land. We might then want to
pick up on the need for an English idyll in the changing world of
the 1930s.

Another contemporary adversarial context is **intersectionality**.
Like ecocriticism, this approach has a long history (again, see
Further Reading), but it is only in recent years that it has become
deployed in literary criticism. We have already seen in Chapter 8
that feminism looks at gender and that Marxism looks at class.
Well, intersectionality is a theory which realises that identity is
more complex than any one perspective can account for. Rather,
identity is constituted at the 'intersection' of a range of categories:
race, gender, sexuality, class, nationality, age, political orientation
and life experience. Intersectionality, then, recontextualises identity in rich and complex ways. It is particularly interested in
understanding the ways that societies use a mixture of these
intersecting categories to *disempower* groups and individuals. An
example we can return to in order to see the kinds of changes this
makes to our reading is the passage where Heathcliff is first
brought to Wuthering Heights, having been found wandering
the streets of Liverpool:

> We crowded round, and over Miss Cathy's head I had a peep at a
> dirty, ragged, black-haired child; big enough both to walk and talk:
> indeed, its face looked older than Catherine; yet when it was set on its
> feet, it only stared round, and repeated over and over again some
> gibberish that nobody could understand.
>
> (25)

In the reading of this passage that I offered in Chapter 5, I was interested in the ways that this was part of Heathcliff's credible continuity.
That is, how key aspects, such as his darkness, were iterated across the
text, but also how other aspects changed, such as his dress and
manner. From an intersectional perspective, I'd focus on how Nelly's
description is the origin of a wider range of elements that, as the novel
will show, are used to oppress Heathcliff. These could include his age,
his poverty, his lack of education, his isolation, his inability to make
himself understood as well as the aforementioned racial markers.
'Heathcliff', in this adversarial close reading, is an *intersection* of those
things. This then becomes our guiding thematic context and, as the
novel progresses, we can see how aspects of his intersectional identity
are developed. The Linton's, for example, pick up on the iteration of
Heathcliff's race, poverty and cultural deprivation:

> 'Oho! I declare he is that strange acquisition my late neighbour made,
> in his journey to Liverpool – a little Lascar, or an American or Spanish
> castaway.' 'A wicked boy, at all events,' remarked the old lady, 'and
> quite unfit for a decent house! Did you notice his language, Linton?
> I'm shocked that my children should have heard it.'
>
> (35)

The Lintons use the intersection of this range of cultural markers
to construct a semantic context for Heathcliff that uses the ambiguous markers race, age, education and class to ostracise him, and to
reinforce a hierarchy in which they are socially superior. Nelly, as
we saw above, takes these markers differently: 'You're fit for a
prince in disguise. Who knows but your father was Emperor of
China, and your mother an Indian queen, each of them able to
buy up with one week's income, Wuthering Heights and
Thrushcross Grange together?' (40). Here Heathcliff's lack of
family, poverty and dark colouring offers romantic possibilities for

his semantic context, but only in fantasy. Heathcliff's reality is one of violent oppression, first delivered upon him and then delivered by him. Taking Heathcliff as an intersection, that is, as a crossover point of a range of categories, offers us a more complex way of appreciating his own thematic 'rise to power'. It's not merely a financial achievement, to be understood, say, through Marxist analysis, it's also one that relates to race, age, gender and education, the structures that disempower him.

THREE FURTHER ADVERSARIAL CONTEXTS

Cognitive poetics is a theory that draws on a neuroscientific understanding of the mind to think about how literature and its interpretation work. One example of this builds on the premise that metaphor is not, as it is most often understood to be, merely a literary or rhetorical form; rather, metaphor is part of the way the mind works conceptually. We fundamentally think – and reason – using metaphor (think of 'left' and 'right' in politics, and the decisions we make based up them). When looking at literature, then, metaphor is far from being unique to literature or poetically novel; rather, literary metaphors are just extensions and elaborations of conventional language. As such, using this adversarial context, we might look at the how a metaphor, such as the 'web' in Jennings' and Whitman's poems (that we looked at in Chapter 6) relates to a conventional metaphor of the 'web' as used in everyday discourse, where a web's basic structure of associations (strength, fragility, complexity, connectivity, a trap, something self-woven, etc.) is often deployed to help us to understand aspects of the world (e.g. the world-wide web). As such, we are fundamentally rethinking the semantic and thematic contexts.

Critical race theory is closely related to intersectionality. One of the main themes of this approach is to examine the ubiquity of racism in a post-civil-rights context where racism may seem less obvious. Why might think, for example, about hidden racist interpretations. For example, a text like *The Great Gatsby* is set in the 1920s' Jazz Age. Gatsby's parties happen to a background of jazz music, but, as Lois Tyson has pointed out, the African American origins of jazz are not considered; indeed, they are rather obscured by the very Europeanised 'Vladimir Tostoff's *Jazz History of the World*' (48). The only significant references to African Americans in the novel are Tom's reading of a racist book, Goddard's *The Rise of the Coloured Races*, and Nick's observations about a party of African Americans that he sees when driving to New York with Gatsby: 'a limousine passed us, driven by a white chauffeur, in which sat three modish negroes, two bucks and a girl. I laughed aloud as the yolks of their eyeballs rolled toward us in haughty rivalry' (64). The 'haughty' black being driven by a 'white' chauffeur seems to fulfil the threat contained in the title of Tom's book, and Nick is prompted to laugh out loud as he dismisses the whole thing, making the African American men animalistic ('bucks') and ridiculous ('the yolks of their eyeballs rolled'). Critical race theory forces us to look at thematic contexts that may appear marginal, or even absent, in a text and recontextualise our interpretation accordingly.

The history of the book considers matters like a book's print history, which as we saw with *Hamlet* and Barrett Browning's sonnets can lead to variant readings. It also considers *who* read the work when it first came out and *how* they read it. Historians of the book also consider what other works were being read at the same time. In the cases of poetry or short stories, a book historian might also be interested in what was published alongside the text in the magazine or paper in which the poem or story appeared as that, they contest, would be part of its context. Each of these would provide a potentially enriching recontextualisation of the actual words on the page, altering the ways in which the inner contexts of close reading are understood.

We can see that some of these adversarial contexts, such as eco-criticism, intersectionality and critical race theory, emerge from contemporary concerns and are crucial to our ability to understand our identities, our place in the world, and to be critical of potentially damaging ideologies and hidden cultural practices. Others, such as the history of the book, arise from a present-day fascination with material culture. Either way, each of these adversarial contexts, and the many others that I haven't mentioned (see Further Reading), open texts to new interpretations, to new ways of being *appreciated*.

Nevertheless, the words on the page and how we read them will always be vital to that appreciation – otherwise why engage with literary texts at all? I would attest that the value of any literary text *as literary* must have at least some relationship to the creative use of language in that text. Therefore, no matter which adversarial context is in place – and there will always be new theories that respond to the priorities of a changing world – the ultimate test of any close reading will be how convincingly it interprets the words on the page, and the methodology presented here will still function as a fundamental critical practice.

FURTHER READING

Peter Barry. 'Ecocriticism'. *Beginning Theory*. 3rd edn. Manchester: Manchester University Press, 2009, 239–261.

Matthew Dickerson and Jonathan Evans. *Ents, Elves, and Eriador: The Environmental Vision of J. R. R. Tolkien*. Lexington: University of Kentucky Press, 2006.

Simon Eliot and Jonathan Rose, eds. *A Companion to the History of the Book*. Oxford: Blackwell, 2009.

Cheryll Glotfelty and Harold Fromm, eds. *The Ecocriticsm Reader*. Athens GA: University of Georgia Press, 1996.

Patricia Hill Collins and Sirma Bilge. *Intersectionality*. Cambridge: Polity, 2016.

Julie Rivkin and Michael Ryan. *Literary Theory: An Anthology*. 3rd edn. London: Routledge, 2017.

Peter Stockwell. *Cognitive Poetics: An Introduction*. London: Routledge, 2002.

Lois Tyson. *Critical Theory Today*. 3rd edn. London: Routledge, 2015.

GLOSSARY

Adversarial context Any theoretical or critical approach that frames the interpretation of a text and thus changes the aspects of its meaning that matter. Examples include Marxism, feminism, **ecocriticism**, psychoanalysis. One of the six **contexts of close reading**. See Chapter 8.

Alexandrine A metrical line of six **iambic feet**.

Alliteration The repetition of consonant sounds at the beginning of words, typically in close proximity (compare **consonance**). This is part of the **iterative context**. In a close reading, alliteration is only important when it is related to other contexts, usually the **semantic, syntactic**, and the **thematic**. See Chapter 6.

Anacrusis The addition of one or more unstressed syllables at the beginning of a metrical line, usually to help the sense.

Anapaest A metrical foot of three syllables, with the stress on the third syllable.

Assonance The repetition of vowel sounds in close proximity within and/or across lines in poetry and prose. This is part of the **iterative context**. In a close reading, assonance is only important when it is related to other contexts, usually the **semantic, syntactic**, and the **thematic**. See Chapter 6.

Caesura A break or pause in a metrical line, typically caused by punctuation or conventional expression.

Consonance The repetition of consonant sounds in close proximity across words (compare **alliteration**). This is part of the **iterative context**. In a close reading, consonance is only important when it is related to other contexts, usually the **semantic, syntactic**, and the **thematic**. See Chapter 6.

Contexts of close reading   See **semantic context, syntactic context, thematic context, iterative context, generic context**, and **adversarial context**.

Credible continuity   An aspect of the **iterative context**, credible continuity is the acceptable range of variations that a character can assume across a narrative and still be believable.

Critical race theory   A contemporary theoretical approach that undertakes to explore the ways in which (often hidden) racism exerts a force in texts and their interpretations. Critical race theory is an **adversarial context**.

Crux   A point in a literary text where two or more of the **contexts of close reading** can be seen to be at work together. These are often points of rich interpretative possibility that will respond to close reading. See Chapter 4.

Dactyl   A metrical foot of three syllables, with the stress on the first syllable.

Ecocriticism   A critical approach to texts that foregrounds landscape, nature, and environment, issues that many critical traditions would normally see as part of the background. Ecocriticism is an **adversarial context**.

End-stopped   A poetic line that ends with a punctuation mark.

Enjambment   A poetic line that does not end in a punctuation mark, the sense of which runs over into the next line.

Foot   The smallest metrical unit in a verse line (see **anapaest, dactyl, iamb, pyrrhic, trochee, spondee**).

Frame metre   The predominant metre for any given poem.

Generic context   The **genre** of a work will typically affect the reader's expectations and range of a work's plausible interpretations, this is its **generic context**. One of the six **contexts of close reading**. See Chapter 7.

Genre   The type of text, e.g. novel, poem, play. Genres are typically broken up into smaller units, or sub-genres, such as tragedy, lyric, gothic, each of which has a range of conventions which will be typical of each member of the group. Genres are rarely pure. See **generic context**. See Chapter 7.

Ground   An aspect of metaphor. The ground is often defined as what the **tenor** and **vehicle** of a **metaphor** have in common. In usage, the ground is typically the aspect of the vehicle that is used to create the novel meaning of the tenor. The ground is often what matters for a close reading. See **metaphor**. See Chapter 2.

Iamb   A metrical foot of two syllables, where the stress is on the second syllable.

Intersectionality   A contemporary theoretical approach that sees identity as made up of an intersection of different factors such as race, gender, sexuality, class, nationality, and age. Intersectionality is an **adversarial context**.

Iterative context   All literary works will contain elements that are repeated, be it sound, rhythm, character, narration or plot elements. These repetitions will be more or less subtly different each time they are encountered by the reader. This repetition with a difference is the **iterative context**. One of the six **contexts of close reading**. See Chapters 5 and 6.

Metaphor   A common linguistic figure where the meaning or meanings of one or more words (**vehicle**) are carried over into the meanings of another word or words (**tenor**), usually creating a new meaning through the connotations inherent in the comparison (**ground**). Compare **simile**. See Chapter 2.

Metonymy   A common linguistic figure that works by using a word or words associated with a thing to refer to that thing. Compare **synecdoche**.

Metre   The repeated patterns of stressed and unstressed syllables in some forms of poetry. In a close reading, metre is only important when it is related to other contexts, usually the **syntactic**, and the **thematic**. See Chapter 6.

Mimetic syntax   An unusual linguistic device where the sentence structure (or syntax) mimics the content of the sentence. More often to be found in poetry.

Narrator   In prose narratives, the narrator is the voice that tells the story. It is typically either a first- or third person voice.

Prosody   The study and analysis of metre and rhythm in poetic works.

Pyrrhic   A metrical foot of two syllables, where neither syllable is stressed.

Quatrain   A four-line section of a sonnet, typically recognisable from the rhyme scheme. A quatrain usually contains a discrete part of the sonnet's meaning or argument.

Rhyme   The repetition of syllables at the ends of lines in proximity in poetry. This is part of the **iterative context**. In a close reading, rhyme is only important when it is related to other contexts, usually the **semantic, syntactic**, and the **thematic**. See Chapter 6.

Rhythm   The pattern made by stressed and unstressed syllables in prose or poetry. In poetry the rhythm may or may not be have an identifiable **metre**. In a close reading, rhythm is only important when it is related to other contexts, usually the **semantic, syntactic**, and the **thematic**. See Chapter 6.

Semantic context   The full range of 'dictionary' definitions and wider cultural connotations of any particular word. This huge range of possible meanings is usually limited by the **syntactic, generic** and **thematic contexts**. One of the six **contexts of close reading**. See Chapter 2.

Sestet   The final six-line section of a Petrarchan sonnet, typically recognisable from the rhyme scheme. A sestet usually contains a discrete part of the sonnet's meaning or argument (see **thematic context**), drawing it to a conclusion (see **sestet** and **volta**).

Sibilance   The repetition of s/z/sh sounds in proximity across a line or lines of poetry of prose. In a close reading, sibilance is only important when it is related to other contexts, usually the **semantic, syntactic**, and the **thematic**. See Chapter 6.

Simile   A linguistic figure in which something (a **tenor**) is given additional meaning by directly comparing it to something else (**vehicle**) using 'like' or 'as' or similar terms (compare **metaphor**).

Speaker   In poetry, the speaker is the voice that the reader imagines for a poem.

Spondee   A metrical **foot** of two syllables in which both syllables are stressed.

Substitution   The replacing of one **foot** with another within a regular metrical line.

Synecdoche   A linguistic figure in which a part of something is used to refer to the whole of that same thing. See **metonym**.

Syntactic context   The ways in which the words in a given portion of verse or prose, usually no shorter than a sentence or longer than a paragraph, will affect each others' meanings. One of the six **contexts of close reading**.

Tenor   In a **metaphor**, the **tenor** is that to which the metaphor is referring. Its meaning will be transformed to a greater or lesser extent by the **semantic context** of the **vehicle**. See **ground**. See Chapter 2.

Thematic context   All texts will contain themes and ideas that develop as the text progresses, and which will guide an interpretation of the text. This is the thematic context. It is a special subdivision of the **iterative context**. One of the six **contexts of close reading**. See Chapters 3 and 4.

Trochee   A metrical foot of two syllables in which the first syllable is stressed.

Vehicle   In a **metaphor**, the **vehicle** is the term which is used to transform the meaning of the **tenor**. See **ground**. See Chapter 2.

Verisimilitude   The realistic qualities of a prose narrative, usually created through everyday details. See Chapter 7.

Volta   The moment in a sonnet where the argument changes, usually indicated by a change in tone and a movement toward resolution.

BIBLIOGRAPHY

PRIMARY TEXTS

Barrett Browning, Elizabeth. *Selected Poems*. Intro. Margaret Forster. London: Chatto and Windus, 1988.

Barrett Browning, Elizabeth. *Aurora Leigh and Other Poems*. Eds. John Robert Glorney Bolton and Julia Bolton Holloway. London: Penguin, 1995.

Brontë, Emily. *Wuthering Heights*. London: Wordsworth, 2000.

Burns, Robert. 'A Red Red Rose'. *The Norton Anthology of Poetry*. Eds Margaret Ferguson, Mary Jo Salter and Jon Stallworthy. 5th edn. New York: Norton, 2005, 759–760.

Cummings, E. E. *Complete Poems: 1904–1962*. Ed. George J. Firmage. New York: Liveright, 2016.

Fitzgerald, F. Scott. *The Great Gatsby*. New York: Scribners, 1953.

Jennings, Elizabeth. *Selected Poems*. Manchester: Carcanet, 1992.

Keats, John. *The Complete Poems*. Ed. Miriam Allott. London: Longman, 1975.

Shakespeare, William. *Hamlet*. Eds Ann Thompson and Neil Taylor. Rev. edn. The Arden Shakespeare. London: Bloomsbury, 2016.

Shakespeare, William. *Romeo and Juliet*. Ed. Brian Gibbons. The Arden Shakespeare. London: Routledge, 1992.

Stein, Gertrude. 'Sacred Emily'. *Geography and Plays*. Boston: Four Seas, 1922, 178–188.

Tolkien, J. R. R. *The Hobbit*. London: HarperCollins, 2001.

Whitman, Walt. *Leaves of Grass and Other Writings*. Ed. Michael Moon. New York: Norton, 2002.

Wordsworth, William and Samuel Taylor Coleridge. *Lyrical Ballads 1798 and 1802*. Oxford: Oxford University Press, 2013.

SELECTED 'CLOSE READING' TEXTS

Barry, Peter. *Beginning Theory: An Introduction to Literary and Cultural Theory*. 3rd edn. Manchester: Manchester University Press, 2009.

Barthes, Roland. *Image, Music, Text*. Trans. Stephen Heath. London: Fontana, 1977.

Barthes, Roland. *S/Z*. Trans. Richard Miller. New York: Farrar, Straus & Giroux, 1991.

Belsey, Catherine. *Critical Practice*. London: Routledge, 1994.

Booth, Wayne C. *The Rhetoric of Fiction*. 2nd edn. Chicago: University of Chicago Press, 1983.

Brooks, Cleanth. *The Well Wrought Urn: Studies in the Structure of Poetry*. London: Methuen, 1968.

Brower, Reuben. *The Fields of Light: An Experiment in Critical Reading*. New York: Oxford University Press, 1951.

Brower, Reuben and Richard Poirier, eds. *In Defense of Reading*. New York: Dutton, 1962.

Cavell, Stanley. *The Senses of Walden*. Expanded edn. San Francisco: North Point Press, 1981.

Childs, Donald J. *The Birth of New Criticism*. Montreal: McGill-Queens University Press, 2003.

Dehane, Stanislas. *Reading in the Brain: The New Science of How We Read*. London: Penguin, 2009.

Empson, William. *Seven Types of Ambiguity*. 2nd edn. London: Penguin, 1961.

Kermode, Frank. *Shakespeare's Language*. London: Penguin, 2000.

Lentricchia, Frank and Andrew Dubois, eds. *Close Reading: The Reader*. Durham NC: Duke University Press, 2003.

Lodge, David. *The Language of Fiction: Essays in Criticism and Verbal Analysis of the English Novel*. New York: Columbia University Press, 1966.

Nowottny, Winifred. *The Language Poets Use*. London: Athlone, 1962.

Pinsky, Robert. *The Sounds of Poetry: A Brief Guide*. New York: Farrar, Strauss & Giroux, 1998.

Richards, I. A. *Practical Criticism*. London: Routledge, 1929.

Richards, I. A. *The Philosophy of Rhetoric*. Oxford: Oxford University Press, 1936.

Richards, I. A. *Interpretation in Teaching*. London: Routledge, 1938.

Ricks, Christopher. *Milton's Grand Style*. Oxford: Oxford University Press, 1963.

Ricks, Christopher. *The Force of Poetry*. Oxford: Oxford University Press, 1995.

Rivkin, Julie and Michael Ryan. *Literary Theory: An Anthology*. 3rd edn. London: Routledge, 2017.

Strachen, John and Terry Richard. *Poetry*. Edinburgh: Edinburgh University Press, 2000.

Tate, Allen. *The Man of Letters in the Modern World: Selected Essays 1928–1955*. New York, Meridian, 1955.

Tyson, Lois. *Critical Theory Today*. 3rd edn. London: Routledge, 2015.

Van Ghent, Dorothy. *The English Novel: Form and Function*. New York: Harper, 1953.

Vendler, Helen. *The Art of Shakespeare's Sonnets*. Cambridge MA: Harvard University Press, 1999.

Waugh, Patricia. *Literary Theory and Criticism: An Oxford Guide*. Oxford: Oxford University Press, 2006.

Wimsatt, W. K. *The Verbal Icon: Studies in the Meaning of Poetry*. London: Methuen, 1970.

Woloksy, Shira. *The Art of Poetry: How to Read a Poem*. Oxford: Oxford University Press, 2003.

INDEX

Glossary entries are indicated by **bold** page numbers.